Manly Piety in Its Principles

Manly Piety in Its Principles

Robert Philip

Waymark Books

Copyright © 2023 by Waymark Books

This is a proofread and newly designed edition of a public domain work.

CONTENTS

1. On Manly Estimates of Both Worlds — 1
2. On Manly Estimates of True Wisdom — 9
3. On Manly Views of Salvation — 19
4. On Manly Faith in Providence — 29
5. On Manly Honesty in Prayer — 38
6. On Manly Views of Divine Influence — 54
7. On Manly Views of Religious Mystery — 74
8. On Manly Views of Divine Holiness — 88

1

On Manly Estimates of Both Worlds

Short as the ordinary term of human life is, it is long enough to justify both the love and pursuit of knowledge, business, and happiness. Neither the shortness nor the uncertainty of our time in this world should be allowed to embitter life, or to cloud its rational prospect. We belong to time as well as to eternity; and it is as much our duty to meet the fair claims of time manfully, as to meet the weighty claims of eternity manfully.

It is no more a man's duty to think only or always of heaven, than it is an angel's duty to think forever of the earth. Angels have both engagements and enjoyments out of heaven, as well as in it. Hence Paul says, *"are they not all ministering spirits, sent forth to minister for them who shall be heirs of salvation?"* But, whatever time or thought their duties on earth may require, their duties in heaven are not neglected. They are interrupted, whenever angels are "sent forth" upon any errand of mercy; but that errand is, itself, just as truly an act of obedience to God, as when they veil their faces in his presence, or strike their harps before his throne. They know that they are doing His will, whether they carry a Lazarus to Abraham's bosom, or swell the hallelujah chorus of the new song; and, therefore, they do both willingly.

In like manner, the duties of life are as incumbent on us as the duties of godliness. We are as much bound to be industrious as to be devotional. It is, therefore, neither a sin nor a shame to feel within us the workings of an active and enterprising disposition, in reference to this world. It is, indeed, both sinful and shameful to feel nothing else. Nothing can excuse or palliate the neglect of "the world to come." The neglect of it is madness, as well as crime. We, ourselves, could not think well of an angel who should prefer to be always out of heaven, even if out on errands of love only. Ministering to the heirs of salvation, is, no doubt, very proper and pleasing work even for angels; but, as it is not the only work they are fit for, or called to; and as it must come to an end, when the world ends, no angel would be justified in setting all his heart upon it, nor in seeking his chief happiness from it. There is before him an eternity of higher and holier engagements; and, therefore, however necessary or pleasant it may be for *"principalities and powers, in heavenly places,"* to learn *"by the church the manifold wisdom of God,"* he would not be a wise angel, who preferred to be always *"sent forth,"* from his place before the throne. And he is certainly not a wise man, who, because there is much to do in the world, and because he likes to be doing, dislikes or neglects to think and act for eternity. Into eternity he can carry nothing of all that he may gain on earth, by worldly pursuits. He is, therefore, laboring for what he must leave forever, forget forever; perhaps curse forever!

"For, what is a man profited, if he gain the whole world, and lose his own soul?" An angel, however often out of heaven, carries with him on his return to heaven the souls he has ministered unto on earth; and their society, through eternity, will be part of his bliss: but the man who lives for time only is fit for hell only; and even to it, he can carry nothing out of this world.

On the other hand, I will readily grant that it would not be creditable to either the talents or the taste of an angel to prefer being always in heaven, whilst there is work to do on earth, worthy of angels and well pleasing to God. Were any of them capable (which they are not) of saying, "I had rather minister to the heirs of salvation as they come into heaven than be sent forth to guard or guide them; and much rather minister before the throne forever than do either;"—this preference, however well meant, would be ill judged. It seems highly spiritual; but it is really selfish. Ministering forever before the throne of God and the Lamb is indeed the highest of all heavenly honors, and the holiest of all heavenly exercises: but, as God and the Lamb take a lively interest in the welfare of the church on earth, and choose that angels should do so too; not to do so—would be disobedience against both divine precept and example, and thus disqualification for ministering at the throne.

Nothing of this kind, however, does or can occur in heaven. Angels are swift as electric flames to do the will of God, whether it call them far within the enshrinements of the eternal throne to adore, or send them forth to the chambers of death to serve. And in both, they are equally happy, although not equally at home; because they find all their happiness in the divine approbation: and that is as much with them when they wait by a death-bed as when they worship at *"the right hand of the Majesty on high."* Such being the sober, although sublime, facts of their case, we are fully warranted to believe that, in our own case, the duties of life are as well-pleasing to God, in their own place and proportion, as the duties of godliness.

It would neither be manly nor godly piety to prefer a life of mere musing, however spiritual, to a life of alternate and blended diligence and devotion. For, if angels do more than meditate and worship, it indicates sloth and weakness rather than high heavenly-mindedness to shrink from industry, or to regret the necessity of labor.

It is, however, arrant mental weakness as well as arrogant impiety to set up the claims of time against the claims of eternity. They only clash when they are made to clash. In themselves they are neither incompatible nor inconsistent. In fact, they are intended and adapted by God to help each other. The cares of this world make the world to come desirable; and the glories of heaven make the glooms of earth tolerable. He, therefore, who lives only for time, levels himself with the beasts that perish. He may build a finer house than the beaver, and amass more stores than the bee, and travel farther than a bird of passage, and rival the butterfly in show, and the nightingale in song: but, if these things engross his soul, and absorb all his time, his rational powers are let down to mere animal instincts; and the results of his life have no more relation to heaven than the songs of a bird or the pursuits of a beast.

Manly eternity does not, then, interfere with the fair claims of time. *"The world to come"* does not interpose its glories or its terrors, to hide or hinder the proper business of this world. Instead of this, the future lends and bends all its high authority to confirm the legitimate claims of the present; making idleness 'worse' than infidelity; hallowing domestic and social love; upholding the sacredness of person and property; and throwing open fields of usefulness to minds of all orders, and to men of all conditions.

Should not, then, the present do equal justice to the future; and time admit and honor the claims of eternity? Oh, it is pitiable, yes, contemptible, to let the things which are temporal divert our whole attention from the things which are eternal. Were any man, under any pretense, to care nothing about the affairs of this life, or to do nothing but mope and muse, we should despise him. Life is not too short for action, nor too uncertain for enterprise. All the faculties and the very form of man, as well as his wants, prove that he was intended for activity. He prostitutes as well as prostrates his rational nature when in a world like this he loves nothing, or lives to no purpose. The sloth of the forest and the slug of the garden reprove such a creature. This censure is as deserved as it is degrading!

Is it the sober fact that a space of time and sphere of action, confessedly narrow, have yet such strong claims upon our regard, that it would be despicable to dispute or evade them. See, then, eternity throw open its interminable duration; its entrancing glories; its unchangeable destinies—shall time be allowed to hide these from us, or to hush up all concern about them? Where is our sensibility or our common sense, if our being engages none of our solicitude? A mote may blind the natural eye; but if a speck of time blind "the eyes of our understanding" to the solemn realities of death, judgment, and eternity, our mental vision must be very weak, or fearfully perverted.

It is despicable indeed, when we, who would not allow the vast expanse of eternity to eclipse the speck of time, allow this speck to eclipse that infinite expanse; flushed as it is with radiant glories or desolate end. There might be some excuse both for our taste and intellect, if we cared too little about this world, and gave the great bulk of our time and thoughts to the world to come; but, to give all to the former, and none, or next to none, to the latter, is utterly inexcusable, and unspeakably paltry. Such a choice, and such conduct, even the devil must despise, however he may be pleased with the fools who persist in it.

Dr. Johnson has well said, "It is only whatever gives the past and the future a predominance over the present, that can raise us in the scale of thinking beings." If, therefore, the present predominate over both, we must even sink on that scale. This is inevitable. There are, indeed, men who rise to the heights of philosophy and poetry by their familiarity with the past. The wisdom of ages is on their lips, and the wealth of history at their command. They are far-sighted in legislation; and all tact in literature. And, could time past return, they, of all men, would be best prepared to mingle with the mighty dead, and to accommodate themselves to the ancient forms and feelings of society. They would be at home with Plato in his taste, and with Homer in his patriotism, and Socrates in his sagacity. But as time past cannot return, this predominance of the past over the future is as irrational as the predominance of the present, because it is equally irrelevant to eternity. I do not underrate such knowledge. He is no ordinary thinker who can amass and apply it. It is, however, no preparation for the society of angels, nor for the fellowship of the general assembly of the spirits of just men made perfect.

The mere antiquary, philosopher, or poet, however high on the scale of intellect, is low on the scale of wisdom if he can prefer an ideal communion with antiquity to real preparation for eternity. Besides, if it be noble to make all the lights of the past bear upon the present, either as beacons to warm, or as lusters to beautify, it must be ignoble and unmanly to let in none of the lights upon the present. Why should they be excluded? The history of time is not so well authenticated as the revelation of eternity. And if the fate of heroes or the fall of empires teach any useful lesson, surely the final destinies of the universe cannot be uninstructive.

Gain, by all means, an acquaintance with former ages. A knowledge of what has been will enable you to appreciate what is; and thus operate as a check on personal vanity and political extravagance. It is, however, what shall be —that alone can prevent you from living for this world, or prepare you for the world to come.

This remonstrance against the neglect of eternal things, and the echoes to it which your own conscience returns, must not be silenced nor disposed of by your intention to look eternity fully in the face, when you are older. Older is an uncertain event. And if it were not so, it is an unmanly excuse. You are old enough to understand, and to act upon, the reasons for looking the claims of this world full in the face. You feel already that you have no time to lose, if you would improve your education or your condition. At least you see clearly how much time and thought would be requisite, in order to realize all that you desire. You ought, therefore, to despise all subterfuges.

"The world to come," is neither a secret nor a mystery. There are, indeed, both secrets and mysteries belonging to it; but, as it offers bliss or woe, it stands out as palpably as the alteration of light and darkness in this world. Indeed, it is far more certain how your principles and character will determine your eternal state, than how they will fix your temporal condition. You may fail to rise in this world, without being to blame; but you cannot sink into hell but by your own fault. You may be disappointed, undeservedly, so far as man is concerned, of settling down in the rank or relationship which you set your heart upon; but you cannot miss heaven if you set your heart upon it. There is no lottery in eternal life, however temporal life may be. In like manner, there is no such mystery about the way of salvation, as renders the experience of old age necessary in order to understand it. There are, indeed, mysteries in the plan of redemption, as well as in nature and providence; but it is not "length of days" that clears them up. It may suit the convenience of the worldly, the idle, and the sensual, to pretend that they know not what to believe: but, whilst they are so dexterous in evading what they ought to obey (about which there is no mystery) it will not be uncharitable to suspect that they see more clearly than they choose to acknowledge how the belief of the gospel would involve obedience. And, what else are your evasions of the immediate claims of salvation and eternity but a betrayal of an unconfessed fact, that you know enough to render your indecision inexcusable?

Yes, indeed; a glass that could concentrate into a focus all the rays of scriptural light which float and flutter around your understanding and conscience; and which should then throw the embodied blaze upon eternity, would startle you at your smiling indecision. For you know that the everlasting song of heaven is redemption through the blood of the Lamb; and, therefore, to take no interest in that song until the evening of life is infamous. You know that without holiness no man shall see the Lord; and, therefore, not to follow holiness until you come to the last stage of the journey of life is base cowardice, or baser rebellion. You know that except you are born again of the Spirit you cannot enter into the kingdom of God; and, therefore, not to pray for the promised and indispensable renewing of the Holy Ghost, or not to yield to His strivings is both ingratitude and insult. And then, what aggravates the whole is that you expect to enter heaven at last, although it be the last thing you now think about, and the least thing in your present estimate of happiness.

How would all this tell at the bar of God when you take your place at His tribunal, it must give "an account" of both the deeds done in the body and of all the motives from which they were done? Well, just try, for a moment, how your present reasons for delay and indecision would bear telling in the presence of God. Perhaps they would not tell well, even to your sister or your mother. You could, of course, make out a case to them, somewhat plausible and satisfactory: but could you submit it to God if you were before God—I mean, if you were before His tribunal, beneath the visible glance of His omniscient eye, with all heaven around you, and the weight of eternity pressing on your spirit—thus you must give in your account.

What, then, is the use of getting up an account to others, which cannot be given in to Him? You would not attempt to pass off upon your mother or your sister the explanations of your indecision, which you would give to a person who knew less of your habits and spirit: and, if your heart condemn you before them, *"God is greater than your heart, and knoweth all things."* You may easily close this book upon this close questioning; but when God's *"books shall be opened"* on the judgment-seat, you cannot close them. The recording angel that opens them, cannot shut them. All that you would conceal, or gladly forget, is registered in them, and will be read to you from them; and the only way in which you can be prepared to hear it all, without being overwhelmed by despair, is by setting your heart at once to seek for a personal interest in the great salvation you are now neglecting.

Perhaps you do not yet see clearly how you could set your heart upon that salvation, without withdrawing it from everything else. But this is quite a mistake. The heart must, indeed, be withdrawn from whatever is sinful; but from nothing that is truly good or rational. The religion of the Bible does not quarrel with the beauties of mature or art; with the wisdom of science or literature: with musical taste, or poetic genius. It forbids and denounces the pursuit of them, as the chief good: but it does anything rather than tie or tame down the mind to despise them. In fact, it exalts and purifies the mind, to enjoy whatever is lovely or useful; and ministers liberally to all that is manly in character, or noble in spirit, or laudable in enterprise.

"A Christian is the noblest style of man," when he is a Christian indeed.

2

On Manly Estimates of True Wisdom

Those who know best the number and character of the ancient systems of philosophy, which successively claimed and obtained the hallowed name of "wisdom," or religion, in Egypt, Greece, and Rome, will least wonder that Paul should brand them with the epithet "foolishness." What else could any man call them, who could say of them, (and defy contradiction whilst he said it) that *"the world by wisdom knew not God."* That could not be wisdom which left God unknown, and immortality undefined. Nothing is religious wisdom that is unable to make man wise unto salvation. Accordingly, no man in the present day, who cares anything about his soul, would be so foolish as to take up with the religious opinions of Plato, Socrates, or Cicero. Even the infidel admirers of these splendid theorists would laugh at any man who should adopt the creed of the wisest of these sages. It was not, therefore, too sweeping nor too severe a charge when Paul called the wisdom of the wisest heathen foolishness. He spoke not of the talents of the ancient philosophers, but of the results of their application. The men themselves were anything but fools. They were the wisest men of their respective nations, and the master-spirits of the world, in all things but religion. Never, certainly, was more power of mind concentrated upon the study of wisdom.

If "searching" could have found out God, or unveiled eternity, they would have made the discovery. But Plato and Socrates failed! And "what can the man do who cometh after" these kings of intellect and imagination? Their systems fell before the gospel, like Dagon before the ark, although the arms of empires upheld them, and the glories of the arts enshrined them, and all the uninspired harps of genius vied in immortal song to immortalize them. The world soon pronounced their wisdom foolishness, when God made Christ 'wisdom" unto man. And now it would be as impossible to make men Platonists in reality, as to make them Druids.

No system has even the appearance of wisdom now, but from the Christianity that is in it. We have therefore no occasion to ask the old question, "Where shall wisdom be found?" For although, as in the time of Job, "the depth and the sea" still say, "it is not in me," and although "destruction and death" can only say, "we have heard the fame thereof with our ears," the gospel says, "it is in me," and proves the assertion true, by pointing to myriads whose character on earth and whose place in heaven demonstrates that they were made wise unto salvation, by applying their hearts to "the wisdom which cometh from above."

Now, thus wise, you desire and hope to be sometime, and by the same means too: for you cannot imagine that the puny dwarfs of modern infidelity can ever depose truths, which the giants of ancient philosophy could not discover: nor can you dream of mightier minds arising to eclipse the reasoning or the research of "the mighty dead." They do not know the meaning of mind (or, with all their talk about the sages of antiquity, they have never studied them) who anticipate from the influence of Voltaire as a wit, or of Hume as a logician, champions of the light of nature, who may do for Deism what the champions of philosophy could not do for it. The mind of the ancients, as mind, like the sculpture of the ancients as art, can never be surpassed in power or splendor.

Christianity has, therefore, nothing to fear, and infidelity nothing to hope, from "the march of intellect." The march of vice, or of mental vacancy, or of vanity, can alone facilitate the designs of sceptics and scorners. Christianity has nothing to dread or deprecate, but inattention to her claims.

I have made these hasty references to the ancients, not so much for the sake of the argument just hinted at, as for the example of attention and application to what was then deemed wisdom. And, surely, if these sages were fascinated and absorbed by mere guesses about God and immortality, the perfect revelation of both deserves our attention. If they bent their mighty minds to the deliberate study of nature, until their hearts burned with the consciousness of power and pleasure, we may well apply ourselves to the study of redemption. Even angels "desire to look into" it, as "the manifold wisdom of God." No wonder.

Redemption flowed from all the perfections of the eternal mind, and from all the sympathies of the incarnate mind. It is the fullness of the Father's grace and the brightness of the Son's moral glory. It is the most mature plan of infinite wisdom, and the loveliest form of infinite benevolence. The silence of the past eternity was first broken by its announcement, and the echoes of the future eternity can never sleep for its celebration. The disclosure of the plan of salvation in heaven, drew around it, as students of the glorious mystery, all the armies of heaven; and the successive revelations of it on earth, made the patriarchs forget their pilgrimages—the prophets their perils—the apostles and martyrs their tortures. This is the wisdom which solicits our attention; and it requires as well as deserves serious and fixed attention.

Neither cherubim nor seraphim, angels nor archangels deem themselves equal to appreciate or understand it without looking into it. The heavenly host bend from their thrones, or burn in their orbit with holy curiosity to comprehend its glories. Yes; and could all the varied knowledge of all the universe be concentrated in one mind, even when all perfect minds are as powerful as the open vision of a completed heaven can render them; that mind would be studious still, and first in zeal and zest for continued and even increasing attention to this wisdom. Still, no wonder.

Redemption by the blood of the Lamb concentrated the entire and intense energies of the infinite mind upon its principles and designs. Omniscience never wearies of watching its progress; nor omnipotence of upholding its claims; nor providence of making all things work together for its good. Emmanuel *"ever liveth to intercede for,"* and the Holy Spirit to help, all who apply their hearts unto this wisdom. Such being the character and claims of the wisdom which maketh wise unto salvation, its own glories might well be expected to win the heart by their own attractions, however the heart was naturally disposed in itself, or solicited by other objects. That which thus draws and absorbs the adoring admiration of beings who need no redemption ought to gain, at once, our confidence and love; for we need all the blessings of that great salvation, which they so greatly admire.

But, alas, we are capable of trifling with eternal redemption, and even inclined to shut our hearts against all its claims. The very utmost that, of our own accord, we are willing to do, is to promise that some portion of the evening of life shall be set apart to meditation and prayer. We have no natural inclination to "number our days" now, in order to apply our hearts now to wisdom. When our days on earth shall be nearly numbered for us, by a power we cannot resist or evade, we see no particular objections to weighing the claims of the gospel; but, at present, we hate the thought of death, and have no natural love to salvation. Whatever we think or feel, at times, differently from this, springs from another source than our own nature.

Look, then, at your instinctive tendencies. They are all against the interests of your soul, and the immediate claims of true wisdom. Even those tastes which are most intellectual and refined prefer human wisdom to divine. This is as unmanly as it is ungodly. A heart thus averse to the great salvation ought to shock and shame you. I am aware that it is easy to expose and upbraid this state of mind; and I know too, that it is sometimes unnecessary to do so. There are moments, when the mind is all thought, and the heart all feeling.

> "The soul, at times, in silence of the night,
> Has flashes—transient intervals of light,
> When things to come, without a shade of doubt,
> In terrible reality stand fully out.
> Those lucid moments, suddenly present
> Glances of truth, as though the heavens were rent,
> And through the chasm of celestial light,
> The future breaks upon the startled sight.
> Life's vain pursuits, and time's advancing pace,
> Appear with death-bed clearness, face to face,
> And immortality's expanse sublime
> In just proportion to the speck of time:
> Whilst death, uprising from the silent shade,
> Shows his dark outline, ere the vision fade;
> In strong relief, against the blazing sky,
> Appears the shadow, as it passes by;
> And, though o'erwhelming to the dazzled brain,
> These are the moments when the mind is sane."
> —Jane Taylor.

This is, however, but the sanity of moments. Such vivid realizations of death could not be kept in habitual combination with real life or godliness. Indeed, they are the warning visions of the ungodly, and not the forms in which death presents itself to believers. You mistake egregiously if you imagine that those who "consider their latter end," are thus convulsed or overwhelmed by the prospect.

No, indeed: those who like Paul, "die daily," like him enjoy life daily. Those who like David, "number their days, that they may apply their hearts unto wisdom," are not terrified by night visions, nor thrown on the rack whenever they realize "the valley of the shadow of death." These starts and storms are the portion of those who "put the evil day afar off." Those who bring it near enough for holy purposes are not haunted by it: for the fear of death, like the keys of death, is under the providential government of the Savior, and thus regulated by His wisdom, as well as alleviated by His grace. In a word, the fear of death is not allowed to embitter or sadden life, when life is consecrated to the service of God.

Were this well weighed, the real connection between the acquisition of true piety and the contemplation of death would cease to appear repulsive. I say, 'the real connection between them' because it is quite different, both in kind and degree, from the relation you imagine them to bear unto each other. When you think of piety, you immediately connect it with the fear of death; and thus the admission of its claims seems to you the admission of a sad and settled fear of dying soon or suddenly; and the bare idea of this is so unpleasant, that, to avoid it, you evade the claims of religion.

You see clearly that you must number your days if you would apply your hearts unto wisdom; but you do not see how wisdom cheers the heart that is applied to it. You forget too, that a Christian has other things to number at the same time with his days. You think of him only as counting them upon the dim dial of suspense: but he is counting too, the number of the great and precious promises of grace; the number of the lovely and lofty prospects of glory; the number of the tender and intense sympathies of his Savior; the number of the sanctifying and consoling influences of the Holy Spirit; and the number of the thoughts, perfections, and purposes of the God of salvation, which are covenanted upon his side.

Oh, there is more to number than "the days of the years of our life." They must be numbered, if we would become wise unto salvation: but then, in applying the heart to that wisdom, we are allowed to number them upon the dial of a special providence, which the unsetting and unshifting "Sun of Righteousness" forever illuminates.

Christians, living as Christians, do not live at the hazard, nor in the suspense you do. You utterly mistake in imagining that, because they do not put the evil day afar off, nor forget their latter end, they thus make the world one vast valley of the shadow of death to themselves; or turn the lights of heaven and earth into sepulchral lamps: or interpret the harmonies of creation as voices from the tomb. No, indeed; this is neither the spirit nor the tendency of the wisdom, which believers learn from Christ: its natural influence is to endear all that is good and lovely in life, and to "turn the shadow of death into the morning" of a glorious immortality. I am neither pretending nor painting whilst saying this. I would, indeed, fain charm you into the habit of considering your latter end; because my heart's desire is that you should be wise unto salvation; but I would not cheat you into the habit.

I will therefore readily, although sadly, allow that you see many Christians in bondage to the fear of death who are anything but cheerful on the pilgrimage of life. This is, however, their own fault. Either they have not sufficiently applied their hearts unto the wisdom of the gospel, and thus missed its strong consolation: or they are indulging some wrong habit or temper, which grieves the Spirit of God: for neither you, nor yet an enemy of the cross of Christ, can point out one feature of the gospel which is in the least calculated to make a Christian gloomy, or to throw a gloom over any thing in life that is really good, or practically useful.

The gospel proclaims free pardon, paternal love, special providence, and certain glory: is there anything gloomy or depressing in these promises? And these are its promises, whatever may be the opinions or expectations of some of its professors. Let them, therefore, be blamed or pitied as their case requires; but do not confound the gospel itself with the confusion of the weak, or with the distress of the inconsistent. This is as unfair and unmanly towards religion, as it is towards taste, to confound the vices of poets with poetry, or the eccentricities of artists with art, or the vagaries of philosophers with science. In understanding, be men.

I repeat it, it is you that live at hazard, and are most liable to the fear and to the stroke of death: for, whilst undecided, you have no security against either. You actually peril your life far more than it is endangered by the ordinary laws of mortality; for by trifling with salvation, and thus tampering with the patience and supremacy of the arbiter of life, you double the risk of a sudden or early death. Ponder this, if you love life, and desire to see many days.

I wish you many happy days; and, because I do so, I tell you plainly that you are placing the life that now is, as well as that which is to come, in a jeopardy, beyond any risk at which believers live. They indeed must die when their time comes; but their "times are in the hands" of their heavenly Father, and their "death is precious in His sight," whereas, your times are in the hands of God as a lawgiver whom you disobey, and as a judge whom you forget: so that, whilst undecided, you have no natural hold upon His forbearance; for you are doing nothing, and caring nothing for anything which He has set his heart upon, or for which He spares life and blesses industry.

True; you have escaped hitherto, and as you feel no symptom of decay, nor see any ominous sign of danger, notwithstanding all your neglect of the great salvation. True also, you see many spared who are as heedless of eternal things as yourself, and not a few grown gray in ungodliness: and I have no wish to hide these amazing facts. They are, however, but one class of the facts which present themselves to our notice. It is a fact that you do not wish to grow gray in impiety: and this settles that part of the matter. And it is also a fact that you could name many who have been cut down as cumberers of the ground, or hurried unexpectedly into death, even since you began to prefer the world to God. They reasoned, just as you do, from appearances, and from probabilities, and from hopes: and now, where are they?

I tell you again, you are periling your life by neglecting godliness. Whilst you stand afar off from the cross and the mercy-seat, you are upon ground which Providence does not watch by pledge or promise. Even the intercession of Christ does not necessarily nor naturally extend to it. If the sweep of His golden censor or the incense of His advocacy embrace at all the neutral ground on which you linger and trifle, you cannot be sure that they shield you; nor can you think that they throw any protection over your life or pursuits, whilst you place no fervent prayers in the censor of the Intercessor.

I dare not let you off yet! There is more implied in these facts than you imagine. Depend on it, there is a gross fallacy in your opinion, or a grand defect in the appeals which are made to you, if you suppose that death stands at the door of piety, either to alarm or to sadden believers. The Savior actually and officially keeps back the hand of death that we may have time to apply our hearts unto wisdom; and He softens the aspect of death that we may enjoy composure whilst trying to become wise unto salvation.

It is not in order to confine our thoughts to death, nor in order to fix them upon the grave, that God binds us to "number our days." He calls for this consideration of our latter end for the sake of a far higher purpose, and of a far happier emotion. God takes no pleasure in human musings about mortality for their own sake; nor does He teach us to try to find pleasure in them. Death is a curse; and, therefore, the author of life and fountain of wisdom teaches no such unnatural lesson as pleasure from contemplating death as death. What He teaches is how the curse may be turned into a blessing, and the natural fear of death blended with a hope full of immortality.

Oh, yes; it is all for the sake of that wisdom by which this is effected that God calls or cares for the habit of numbering our days. He knows perfectly, and we too know well, that whilst we banish all thought of dying, we can banish all the claims of salvation: and that whilst we refuse to number our days, we shall not number our mercies nor our responsibilities; and, therefore, He teaches this moral arithmetic.

Besides, and I adjure as well as beg you to remember it, the gospel is the word of eternal life and therefore it will only treat with man as an heir of eternity. It is not chiefly because we may not live long in this world that the gospel is so urgent and authoritative in its appeals; but because we cannot "live always" in this world. Eternity is inevitably before us! There is the real reason for pressing on us the duty of keeping in sight the end of time.

God's object is not to vex, nor to pain, nor to terrify us, but to inspire us with the sublime consciousness of our own mortality that we may spring up from the trammels of days and years to lay hold on eternal life. He wants man to be manly in godliness; and, therefore, He treats him as a man; and that with god-like solemnity and father-like tenderness. In a word, He as much consults our happiness when He sets us to number our days, as when He crowns our days with health and prosperity: for as the latter are intended to furnish us with opportunities of becoming wise unto salvation, so the former is intended to enforce and secure the improvement of these opportunities. Remember, them, the real connection of death with religion: godliness has the promise of this life, as well as of that which is to come.

To all of whom it can be truly said, *"Ye are Christ's,"* God says, *"All things are yours, whether life or death."* It is therefore unmanly to confound the vulgar motions, which are afloat on this subject, with the spirit of the gospel. That is not only opposed to all gloomy ponderings about death, but full of securities for life, as well as for salvation. No man has such a hold upon the tenure of life, or is so far beneath the shadowing wing of providence, as the man who lives unto God; because God has great purposes to carry on in the world by godly men; and, therefore, He takes a special interest in sparing them, whilst His work wants them. It does not, indeed, want some of them so long as we imagine; but, as it will always go on by instrumentality; life must be always safest in his service.

In a word, life can have no moral securities, apart from godliness.

3

On Manly Views of Salvation

Amongst the many points of view in which the oracles of God exhibit the salvation of the soul; that is at once the most splendid and profound which represents it as "the life" of the soul. *"Hear, and your soul shall live,"* was the appeal with which the prophets opened or closed their messages of mercy from God to man. *"He that believeth on me shall have everlasting life,"* was the grand motive by which the Savior commended the claims of the gospel. Now, no familiarity with this view of salvation should be able to hide from you the sublimity or the glory of the promise and prospect of the eternal life of the soul.

The life of the body may be periled by sin and cut short in judgment; but sin can never rouse judgment against the vitality of the soul: for devouring fire cannot consume it, nor "the worm that dieth not" waste it. It is not, therefore, natural immortality, or living forever, that the oracles of God set before us, when they propose to us the eternal life of the soul. It is, therefore, the well-being of the soul that is called its life, by the scriptures: and this being the fact of the case, it can commence now, as well as continue forever; for the well-being of a soul cannot be so dependent on circumstances as to be impossible out of heaven. It cannot, indeed, be perfect out of heaven, because the human soul is both imperfect in its faculties and unholy in its affections: but, as the happiness of heaven will consist in the perfection of knowledge, character, and safety, the present happiness of the soul must be attainable here, just in proportion to the degree in which we acquire part of the same knowledge—part of the same character—part of the same safety, which are enjoyed there in perfection.

Now these sources of the soul's well-being are not confined to heaven. It is as possible to obtain some holiness here. The safety of the soul on earth may be rendered as certain as the stability of an angel in heaven. And, as revealed Godhead is the same—in essence, character, and will—as unveiled Godhead—much of the same knowledge, which is the bliss of glorified spirits before the throne, may be learned on the footstool, and thus be the source of some real blessedness to the soul now.

Nothing is more irrational or unscriptural than the hollow notion that heavenly blessedness is confined to heaven. So far indeed as it consists in entire and eternal exemption from all natural and moral evil, it is all within "the gates of the new Jerusalem:" but so far as this beatific vision is intellectual, glimpses of its glory flash over the walls of the celestial city and shine down upon this world. The revealed fact that God is love is just as true here as that fact unveiled is transporting there; and, therefore, it can produce in us some of the same joy.

The revealed fact that the Lamb slain can save unto the very uttermost because He ever liveth to intercede, is just as true here as the sight of His intercession is inspiring there; and, therefore, the belief of it must give some of the happiness which is created by the sight of it. In a word, however much more and better God and the Lamb are known by the general assembly in heaven, they are known in no different character from that in which they are revealed on earth. They are not different beings on the eternal throne from what they are in the everlasting gospel. It is, therefore, in degree, not in kind, that the spiritual happiness of heaven differs from the joy and the peace which springs from believing the truth concerning salvation.

Let, therefore, no slothful or sluggish mind divert your attention from the sublime fact (for it is as sober as it is sublime) that the eternal life of heaven may begin now; nor from the solemn fact that it must begin here if the soul would live forever in heaven. Eternal life there is the continuation of loving and serving God here. "The second death," is the sad end which comes of disliking and disobeying God. Neither heaven nor hell will be new, the trajectory of both begins here Both virtue and vice are now the foretastes, in some measure, of what they "shall be:" for the former *is "the savor of life unto life"* and the latter *"the savor of death unto death."* Such being the solemn facts of the case, you ought never to think of heaven without at the same time thinking of the absolute necessity of spiritual life now. It is mere trifling with the great salvation to regard the gift of eternal life as something altogether in the next world. It never can be a future blessing to you unless you obtain the principle and hope of it as a present blessing; for it is as much intended by God for present use as for future enjoyment—to bless in the current time as to beatify eternity; to improve this world, as to perfect the world to come.

On the other hand, never think of the necessity of immediate spiritual life without at the same time thinking of a glorious future to come. Always look at eternity, when you sit down to weigh the present claims of godliness; for as mere duties, devotion, self-denial, circumspection, and prudence will not always enforce themselves by their own native influence. Not, however, that their innate excellence is insufficient to commend them; for they are worthy of all attention: but because the world can easily upset their claims. It can, alas, too readily, make out a case against godliness, even when the light of eternity is let in upon duty and devotion. Things that are seen and temporal will therefore carry the point against piety unless the things which are unseen and eternal are kept in view: for it was only whilst he "looked" at the latter, that Paul even could keep the former in their own place. There must, therefore be a frequent recognition and realization of what you intend to be forever—to do forever— to try forever—to feel forever in heaven— if you would do, feel, or be, on earth what becomes and behooves an expectant of glory.

To leave your character to be shaped by circumstances or modified by accident will no more prepare it for the inheritance of the saints in light, than the waves of the sea will lash the rocks on the shore into forms of life and loveliness. The action of events upon the character may alter it somewhat for the better: but not at all according to the model of the Divine image: circumstances can no more work out a likeness to Christ than the stormy waves can chase the rude rocks into the symmetry and truth which followed the chisel of Phidias and Canova. *"Ye must be born again"*—if you would enter the kingdom of heaven; and you cannot be born again of the Spirit of God unless you allow the word of God to bring the great salvation before your mind, just in the light which Christ presented it—radiant with the glory or filled with the gloom of destruction. This is its real aspect in the Bible. It embraces time, but it is based on eternity. It does not forget that we are mortal; but it woos and warns us by spirit-stirring appeals: the promise of immortality.

Your, soul, then, needs nothing less than eternal life; and it can only inherit that in heaven by acquiring a title and fitness for heaven now. Do you believe this? However that may be, no one understands this, agreeably to the revelation of the fact, who disbelieves that sin has brought the sentence of *"the second death"* upon his soul, and the seeds of spiritual death into his soul. Do you think this *"a hard saying,"* to apply to yourself, or a harsh construction to put on your condition as a sinner? If so, if indeed you have any suspicion of its being so, do not blink it. Bring out all the suspicion and dislike which you really feel: for you can make nothing useful of the gospel until you want its grace to take off the curse of the law from your soul, and to quicken your soul into spiritual life. It is all lost time and labor to apply to Christ for anything less than deliverance from *"the wrath to come;"* or to apply to the Holy Spirit for anything less than a *"new heart."* Remember, it was to *"seek and to save the lost,"* that Emmanuel came into the world and poured out his soul unto death. He died, that we might live.

You might therefore just as well say that He did not die for sin as think that you are not dead, in law, by sin. If you do not deserve the wrath of God, why did He endure the wrath of God? If you are not under the curse, why was He made a curse for you? Can your dislikes stand out in the face of these questions? Can you even doubt, for a moment longer, whether you are exposed to the second death? For do you not see that if you maintain that you are not condemned by the law, you cannot even imagine that Christ died to justify you by grace? In like manner, cavils against the deadness which the influence of sin has produced on the soul are in fact cavils against the work of the Holy Spirit; for if no moral death has affected the powers and passions of your soul, you are not a subject for divine operations. They begin by quickening the soul; and *"it is the Spirit that quickeneth:"* so that you actually cut yourself off from the very source of spiritual life whilst you question the fact of spiritual death in your own case.

Such solemn considerations are, I am aware, almost a temptation to believe anything, however bad, of ourselves rather than risk the tremendous consequences of running directly in the face of the work of the Son and the Spirit. Indeed, I would not have ventured to bring the matter to such a startling point, without more prefacing, had I not the prospect of leading you through this subject step by step, and enabling you, thus, to judge for yourself more calmly than a strong appeal will allow. I must content myself in the meantime, however, with simply telling you that all your aversion to divine things is just the deadening effect of sin upon the soul; and that it is just as sure that the curse of the law has passed upon your soul as that you have broken the law. You may not feel it now any more than you feel it on your body; but the sentence of death is upon both. How can you, then, imagine that your soul is not under it, seeing your body is under it? But for sin, the body had never been liable to temporal death; and as that cannot touch the soul, the second death is the sentence of the law on the soul.

Here, then, is a predicament of responsibility and peril that may well awaken in your soul the piercing cry, "What shall I do to be saved? What shall I do to inherit eternal life?" Now, what do you think ought to be done that your soul may live unto God here and with God hereafter? You have, of course, heard and read enough of the gospel to be aware that the proper answer to this question is, *"Believe in the Lord*

Jesus Christ, and thou shalt be saved." Well; does that answer at all relieve your fears? Salvation is by faith in Christ: does that bring it any more within your reach than if it were by works? What do you think you can make of believing for everlasting life? What do you intend to try; when you shall attempt to exercise faith on Christ for salvation? What is faith? What ought you to believe about Christ? Why is believing made the first thing, and the only thing, required in order to obtain life?

I multiply these questions not to confuse you, but to bring before you all the confusion which exists in your own mind on this subject. These questions could not confuse you, if you understood the subject. Let them therefore set you to define to yourself what you mean by faith. Tell yourself what you really suppose it to be, and what you intend to do when you try to believe.

Well; what do you think of faith? I suppose I may safely say for you, that you regard it as "some great thing" which you would be very glad to possess, but which you hardly know how to obtain. I hope I may add to this, that you regard it as the gift of God; as the fruit of the Spirit; and thus as a holy principle of love and obedience. No believing is true faith which has not this character and spirit.

Well, now; how do you propose to obtain this precious faith? Here, perhaps, is your chief difficulty. You see what the principle of faith ought to be and to do; but how to acquire it is the question. Yes! And it is a very solemn question. We must, however, keep our senses amidst all its solemnity if we would arrive at any sober-minded conclusion. What, then, do you think of trying in order to obtain saving faith? Perhaps you have not made up your mind on this point yet. You see that, in some way, the gift of faith must come from God; and feel as if you must wait until He implant the principle in your heart. I mean by waiting what you mean: not utter idleness nor inattention, but waiting in the use of means. This is your plan; and, should you on some happy day feel this precious faith springing up in your heart, you intend to exercise it very freely and fully upon the Savior: but, until you feel something of it, how can you (as you say) exercise it?

Now I think, I at length, understand you; and you are not displeased to see that when your ideas are put into words, there is more clearness and connection in them than you at first expected to find. It is also rather gratifying to find that you are not twitted as if you were utterly ignorant or indifferent on the subject. I have, indeed, charged you with confusion on the point, but I have given you credit both for solicitude and sincerity. Well; will you give me credit for equal sincerity, when I tell you that however well you mean, you quite mistake the way in which believing the gospel gives life to the soul? It is not faith itself that gives life; but the Gospel which is made the means of faith and life too, at the same time, by the Spirit of God.

You will understand this distinction if you will substitute for the word "believe" another scriptural word which is equally connected with the promise of salvation. I mean the word "hear." God says expressly, "Hear and your soul shall live." Now you misunderstand the gospel sadly if you do not see that what you hear in it is the only thing there is to believe, or from which life can be obtained. What the gospel says is the source of faith and hope too; so that if what we hear from it does not comfort us, faith cannot comfort us; for there is nothing to believe but just what is said. Looking out to the gospel for truth, and not looking into the heart for faith, is, therefore, the way to obtain salvation. All the hope, all the encouragement God gives to us is in what He tells us of his mercy in Christ Jesus. It is by "glad tidings," that He gladdens the heart; and, therefore, it is only in listening to them, and in welcoming them as such, that the Holy Spirit renews the heart.

Let no one confuse you on this matter: there is nothing in faith itself, but believing; and there is nothing to believe but just what God says. What else could there be, seeing that *"faith cometh by hearing, and hearing by the word of God?"* It is indeed, *"the fruit of the Spirit:"* but, let the Eternal Spirit Himself tell you how He produces it. *"The Holy Ghost saith, to-day if ye will hear my voice."* Remember also, how the Savior summed up, in his apocalyptic appeal, all His ministerial lessons on the office of the Holy Spirit: *"He that hath an ear let him hear what the Spirit saith unto the churches."* This is teaching to profit! Here we are solemnly and authoritatively summoned away from all idle and vague wishing for the work of the Spirit to give immediate heed to the word of the Spirit, if we want to experience his influences. This is an intelligible process for becoming wise unto salvation by faith in Christ Jesus. It is also a testing process.

A man may flatter himself that he is very willing to be a true believer, so long as he regards faith only as a grace or a gift he has to wait for; but let him fairly meet the claims of the gospel on his immediate attention; and mark impartially how he likes to hear it seriously—to read it prayerfully—to ponder it deeply, to submit to it meekly, and act on it honestly, so far as he understands it—and he will soon see the real state of his heart before God, as well as discern the mighty difference there is between waiting for a gift and seeking for one.

The sober fact of your case is that you desire faith as much as you delight to acquaint yourself with the way of salvation; and no more than you are concerned about your own salvation. The real degree of your willingness to be indebted to grace for the gift of faith is just the degree of your willingness to give *"good heed"* unto the things which belong to your everlasting peace. If you are not inclined to lay them to heart now, you are not willing to be a believer now nor are you yet waiting for faith. You are, in fact, standing idle, in a place, a position, and a spirit to which that gift of God is not promised.

Hear the Spirit, if you would have the Spirit to help you! Show that you prize and long for His renewing work on your heart by listening with deep attention to His word concerning all that Christ has done, and all that God in Christ is. This is the truth—to be believed. It is to give this truth the force of truth on the mind that the Holy Spirit works and witnesses. And, what glorious truth it is. Well may it be *"the incorruptible seed"* by which men are born again of the Spirit, and from which He raises the harvest of faith and holiness. Oh, hear it for yourself and by yourself! Retire alone with God, and listen to Him as if He spoke to you only. You have not given Him a fair hearing in public if you have not thus listened to Him in secret. You have hearkened to the gospel only as a system of doctrine, or as a scheme of duty, and not as the heaven-sent message of mercy and grace to your soul, if you have not gone alone with God, to hear it again, as from His own lips.

Is it necessary to say to you that the gospel is worth hearing; or to ask you whether you ever set yourself to hear it as the glad tidings of God's good will to your soul. You have, of course, listened to gospel-sermons and compared one sermon with another, and, perhaps, compared them all with their texts, and with the tenor of Scripture. So far well. But this is not hearing that your soul might live; that you might know what God feels for you; that you might see your own way and welcome to escape from the wrath to come. You have listened and heard; and, no doubt, with some desire to get good from the gospel. You may even have felt at times that you were profiting under it; and seen very clearly how great good might be derived from it. But, pause now, and meet this one simple question: what do you really mean by getting good under the gospel? What good do you expect? One thing you mean is, of course, that you yourself should grow better in heart and character. So far well. Nothing can do us real good unless by making us really good. That is the practical design of all that God has said to us in the gospel. He begins, however, by doing us good, in order to make us good. He doeth us good at once by the gospel itself; for the moment a man hears it as "good news," he gets good from it, and continues to get good from it while he continues to hear it as good news. No man can hear it as good news without getting good from it; for it gives hopes at once—encouragement at once—by warranting an immediate application to God for mercy. This is not, indeed, all the benefit it begins with; but, without this, nothing else could do us good.

You are, therefore, not thoroughly in earnest about salvation; or, like "the heath in the desert," you "know not when good cometh," if what you hear in the very first appeals of the gospel to you, fail to do you good: for as it opens with the express assurance that "God is in Christ reconciling the world to Himself," you must be unwilling to be reconciled yet, or you are not fully aware of your need of reconciliation. That—you do need, however, as much as you need to grow better. Indeed, you never can improve in character before God until your heart is right with God; and right it will not be made by the Spirit of God until you take the word of God for all the mercy and grace you require.

4

On Manly Faith in Providence

Of all the pompous inanities of a "talking philosophy," the most contemptible is the pretense that the greatness and grandeur of the universe renders the affairs of this world, and especially of individuals, too insignificant to be regulated by a special Providence. Because, forsooth, the solar system is immense, and systems of suns magnificent, and space as brilliant as boundless, some argue that man is too mean to be an object of divine solicitude, or of providential care. The men who talk thus profess to be influenced by lofty ideas of God, and by a sacred regard to His majesty. They say that it is both vulgar and presumptuous to imagine that the Great Supreme should notice little things, or interfere with the course of human affairs. It may be worthy of Him, they allow, to sustain the great laws of nature, and to superintend the universe as a whole; but to hear the prayers or heed the conduct of individuals, they deem unworthy of God. Thus they profess to exalt the Deity. There is, however, nothing so vulgar as this in all the common motions of Providence. The language of this theory is fine; but the principle of it is coarse, and the spirit of it mean, and its whole aspect more degrading to Deity than the lowest notion of His providence, which the weakest Christian entertains. For, this theory confines the attention of the mind to the mindless parts of creation—to masses and motions of mere matter; whereas, the most vulgar theory of Providence places God in the province of life and mind—a sphere which has some resemblance to Himself, and with which He can hold some rational intercourse, or feel some natural sympathy. Suns and systems and all the vast machinery of the universe have no affinity with the divine nature, and no consciousness of the divine care; and therefore to make them the sole or the chief objects of divine attention is to degrade God. They are, indeed, immense and magnificent; but, in themselves, they are as base as they are bulky, and as inert as they are innumerable. How, then, can that be an exalted idea of God, which confines his care and complacency to mere machinery, and excludes from both, beings capable of knowing and enjoying both?

Oh, the grossest superstition was never so vulgar; as this vapid refinement superstition has always, at least, represented the Infinite Mind as occupied about mind, and as subordinating matter to the improvement of spirits; and, although sometimes too familiar (and at other times too fanciful) in its details of Providence, it was never so brutish as to fill the heart or hands of Deity with machinery. It remained for men, calling themselves "philosophers," to do this. And most fully have they verified the apostolic proverb by it; *"professing themselves to be wise, they became fools."* This sarcasm is not too severe, even if these refiners regard every star in space as an inhabited world, and all the inhabitants as perfect beings. That is, certainly, a splendid conception, and as probable as it is sublime. It was most likely this view of the universe, which compelled David to exclaim, *"What is man, that thou art mindful of him; or the son of man, that thou visitest him?"* The holy amazement which breathes and burns in this exclamation, must be shared by everyone, who, like David, *"considers the heavens"* in this light.

The moment we vividly realize to ourselves a boundless universe teeming with brighter worlds and higher orders of beings we begin to see their countless claims upon the notice of God, and to hear the sphered harmony of their worship, and to feel the superiority of their nature; and thus to find our own level. So we ought. It is, however, the brute on the devil's level, which that man sinks to, who concludes that God cares nothing about mankind: for it is just as likely that God should care for men as for angels. He *"humbleth Himself,"* when he condescends to *"behold the things which are in heaven,"* as well as when He watches over the earth. The highest seraph is not so much above the lowest creature as he is beneath the Creator. As, therefore, the Creator does condescend, even when he rules amongst the armies of heaven, nothing can disprove His rule amongst the inhabitants of the earth: for there is no such difference between angelic and human beings as to render the government or the guardianship of man unworthy of God. We are, indeed, utterly unworthy of such a Providence, and especially of such Grace, as He exercises on our behalf; but, as both are exercised for the express purpose of training up human spirits to angelic perfection and eternal felicity, both are just as worthy of God, as is the moral government of the unfallen universe. Dr. Chalmers, if he has not exhausted this subject in his Astronomical Discourses, has embodied it in forms of power and glory, which fascinate equally the understanding and the imagination.

It is not, however, in this department of the question that the disbelievers in a special Providence unmask themselves fully. It is when prayer is proposed as the means of averting or mitigating the calamitous visitations of Providence. Then the disbelievers show themselves in their true colors and meet the proposal with sneers or sophisms. I say "the proposal for public prayer" for by the time that is carried into effect throughout the nation, the calamity that calls for it has either created a public voice which drowns the hissing of sceptics, or made them "believe and tremble." The recent visitation of pestilence in this country had this effect. Whilst that calamity hovered on the confines of the land, or only swept through the lanes of vice and wretchedness, the witlings of the senate and the leviathans of the press vied with each other in ribaldry and fool-hardiness. Prayer and humiliation were put upon a level with the hurdle-fences, which someone was said to have placed around his farm for protection. But when the crisis came, and "the high places" of the earth in common with the lowest were perilous; and when the sound heart of the nation sent the nation to its knees, even infidels were awed into silence.

Journals that had never named Providence before except to ridicule it, and never referred to God except by swearing, slipped into their leading articles, from time to time, such admissions of both, as betrayed their own alarm. The cravens of that crisis may choose to forget this fact; but history will not forget that they trembled quite as much as the men who fasted and prayed then.

Fears, I am fully aware, do not establish facts, however they may illustrate them. Let us, therefore, look at the argument against the use of prayer, as it is put forward, before the fluttering of the heart make the lips falter, or the spirits sink. Its validity, if it be valid, should not be judged, whilst its authors are almost frightened out of their wits by physical danger. Well; it is this: that as famine, pestilence, and all kinds of peril, have, of course, natural causes, their removal or mitigation, in answer to prayer, would involve a violation of the great laws of nature. This is really great nonsense; but as it is called philosophy, and is sometimes gravely treated by true philosophers, we must, I suppose, notice it. Now, certainly, a violation of the great laws of nature is a very solemn matter. But, what law (great or little) of nature requires to be altered or relaxed, even for a moment, in order to make room for the influence of prayer? When prayer is for life or health, there may be moral causes why God should not vouchsafe to answer it; but there can be no natural causes to prevent Him, even when the atmosphere is charged with pestilence. Even then, He has no occasion to neutralize the natural effluvia that floats around us, nor to direct its currents from our path, in order to preserve us: He has only to will the continuance of our moral probation as "space for repentance" or as opportunity for service; and life is sure, the end is gained, without touching a law or a wheel of the universe. It is not by any, nor by all these laws, that the soul is accountable. Moral laws alone can effect the term of its probation: and if they require it to be either prolonged or shortened, nothing in the course of visible or invisible nature can prevent it. The probation of the man, and the course of nature, go on together. Thus all that requires to be done, in order to the continuance of life, is to continue the soul as a candidate for eternal life; then, disease, however prevalent or pestilential, can no more dislodge the probationary spirit, than it infects the angelic spirits who move and minister among the death-beds of the heirs of salvation.

This, I am aware, is argument, only to those who believe the revealed responsibility and probation of man. With those who do not, it will go for nothing. True: but it makes their assumption of the Christian name, and their protests against the name infidel, go for nothing. Thus, if it prove nothing to them, it proves much concerning them. It does not convince them of the truth as it is in Jesus; but it convicts them of hypocrisy, in pretending to pay homage to Christianity; and thus unmasks to you the men who mock at prayer, and equivocate about providence. Those secret disbelievers who have discernment enough to see this, and selfish reasons for evading detection, shelter themselves under the acknowledged cessation of miracles; and parry off argument from general principles, by asking, whether we expect God to work a miracle for our preservation when we pray in times of danger? This also is a paltry subterfuge.

There is nothing but empty sound in the talk about the natural connection between cause and effect, when life is periled by peculiar diseases. In some states of the atmosphere, the cause of disease is equally present to all who are under the same meridian; but it does not produce the same effect, even upon all who are of the same temperament and habits. One is taken, and another left. Some die; many suffer; and more escape. Now, although it would be unwise to call the escape of the many a miracle, it is unquestionably in consequence of the natural effect not following the natural cause, in their case. They inhaled, unhurt, or with 'little injury, the same air which proved fatal to their compeers in age and circumstances. The Christian ascribes this exemption of the many, to a special providence, which spares them for the probation of grace or of glory; and thus he gives both a sufficient and a sublime reason for the event: but, to what can the infidel ascribe it? He has no general principle to resolve it into, which can explain it. His great general principle that cause and effect follow each other inevitably and invariably, it gives the lie to, so far as life and death are concerned. And as to what is called accident and chance, these are things which, however he may talk of them in order to avoid answering awkward questions, are as incompatible with his system as miracles, or an extraordinary providence.

Dr. Chalmers has grappled with the infidel philosophy of our time, on this subject, in his own way: and, as I am not aware that he has published his argument yet; and as the report I have of it, is not unlike himself, I will embody the substance of it:— "Observation carries us a certain way along the chain of causes and effects: but above our loftiest ascent there are other phenomena, which we vainly try to reach. So it is in all philosophy. After reaching the highest ascertainable causes, there are others still higher, which distance all our powers of research; and a wide region beyond all our investigation, of which we can positively say nothing. It may be under the control of higher beings in the universe; or nature may be like a chain, of which a few lower links are visible: but the upper link of which, is appended to the throne of a prayer-hearing and prayer-answering God. It may be by a responsive touch at a higher part of the chain than is within our observation that prayer meets with its answer. It is not amidst the seen and visible causes where it would be a miracle; but by an unseen, though not less efficient, touch amongst the remote causes, that God answers prayer. If it be in the latter way, there may well be a providence, as special as the wants of His dependent family, without at all infringing on the constancy of the course of nature. If the responsive touch were given within the sphere of observation, then the answer would be a miracle, or a contravention of the known laws of nature. But if it be without the sphere of observation, then the answer may be as effectual, without any violence to any sequence of visible nature.

The reaction of the answer strikes at a higher part of the chain, than we see: not by a visible movement in the experimental region below, but by an invisible movement in the transcendental region above. It is there—that the Supernal Power of the universe, the Cause of causes, puts forth an influence, which is propagated downwards to the lowest extremity of the chain; and thus He carries forwards events in answer to prayer, without disturbing the visible mechanism of nature. It is thus we live under the care of a presiding God, and yet amid all the regularities of a harmonious universe.

"But instead of treating it as a general argument, let us take some individual examples. When the sighing of the midnight storm sends a fearful agitation into the mother's bosom, as she thinks of her sailor-boy, tossed on the tempestuous deep, the advocates of a hard and inflexible constancy in nature would forbid her to pray. According to them, prayer to the God who holds the elements in his hand is as useless as to the elements themselves. Yet nature strongly prompts her aspirations for the safety of her boy; and, if our argument be true, there is nothing in science to repress them. God can answer her, not by interfering with second causes, or reversing the changes of the heaving atmosphere; but by a touch of his hand amidst the deep recesses of meteorology. Thus, He might bid the elements into silence. A virtue passes out of Him, which passes onward from the invisible to the visible." This is, emphatically, meeting the objectors on their own ground, and foiling them with their own weapons; for they hold no philosophical ground or weapons, if they refuse to admit that even science sees only the lower links of the chain of causes and effects.

And yet, after all, this splendid and profound argument just comes to this, "that nothing is impossible with God." Thus the real philosopher and the real Christian, meet at the same point, and rest on the same principle.

To those, however, who believe Christianity, (and no one does so who disbelieves the redemption of sinners by the atonement of the Lamb of God) the reign of grace, presents both the most satisfactory proof and explanation of a special providence. For, without such a providence as can prolong life, and preserve health, for all the purposes which God is covenanted to carry on in the world by the instrumentality of the church, there could be no moral security for the reward of Christ, or the salvation of man. Life, health, and reason must have some providential securities, if men are to be trained up for heaven, and heaven eventually peopled from the earth. All the laws of nature must be subordinate at all times to the designs and laws of grace, so far as grace requires time and opportunity to do its work on the heart and character.

Now, neither that time nor that opportunity is provided for to a certainty, by the course of nature. Much of both is, indeed, certain from the order and uniformity of that course, not enough without providence. Pestilential vapors generate from time to time, and spread so widely, that if they wasted life or health according to the abstract law of cause and effect, a city, yea, a nation, might perish in a day!

It is, then, providence we live under; and its great object is to promote the designs of the gospel. As sure, therefore, as you are under the gospel, you are also under both the care and correction of a special providence. You can neither sin with impunity, nor suffer by accident. Your own history illustrates and proves this already. Yes; you have met with some checks or chastisements, which made you feel, if not confess, that the eye of God had been upon your heart and habits. Certain trials were no mysteries to you, whatever they seemed to others. You had a key to their secret cause, and knew well the real connection between your sin and your punishment. In fact, you suspected at times, how certain lines of conduct would end, and were not so much surprised at the issue as you were pained by it. You are not singular in this experience. All smart, more or less, for their misconduct, however few acknowledge the retribution. And, if you will keep your eyes open and fixed upon the discipline of providence, as it goes on in the church of God, you will often be struck with the peculiar suitableness of certain dispensations, to the character of certain individuals. This may be frequently seen even in the world: but, in the church, it is always to be seen. There, a process is forever going on, which answers, in a great measure, all the practical purposes of the ancient miraculous gift of "discerning spirits:" character finds its level, and principles their test, and thus men are brought out in their true colors, in the long run, by the touch of a discriminating providence.

Only wait and watch, in the case of those who cloak sin or selfishness under the garb of religion; and you are sure to see them exposed or improved eventually, by "the mighty hand of God." I am not teaching you to be spies, nor yet to be interpreters, in the case of others; but still I say, keep your eyes open and intent on the wheel of providence, if you would keep your own conscience in a healthy state. The expected exposure of the hypocritical and heartless can be no pleasure to you; and, therefore, you can hardly be too silent when they are detected; but neither can you be too observant: it will tell well on your own character, to mark how their "sins find them out." My own attention was drawn early to this maxim; and often and awfully have I seen it verified.

Truly did Christ say, *"If a man abide not in me, he is cast forth as a branch, and is withered; and men gather them, and cast them into the fire." "Every branch in me that beareth not fruit, my Father taketh away."* I tell you again, you cannot sin with impunity, nor without detection. Providence will way-lay your movements, however secret they may be; and expose you to the world, at some point of them, where you least suspect and can worst afford to be found out. Remember too, that whilst providence thus unmasks the sensual and the fraudulent, it also takes effectual measures against "the lusts of the mind," as well as against the lusts of the flesh. Pride is sure to be brought low, and vanity to be mortified, and ambition to be checked, and imprudence to be chastised. Look around you, and see if they are not. What "thorns in the flesh," or "crooks in the lot," or "crosses on the shoulder," are visible in the church, wherever pride of intellect, person, or office, is a besetting sin?

Verily there is a God that judgeth! Do not, therefore, provoke the Lord to jealousy; for he will "visit transgression with rods."

5

On Manly Honesty in Prayer

However familiar we may be with the idea of retiring for secret prayer to God, or of meeting for social prayer, the first persons who did so for the first time must have felt it to be a very solemn and sublime exercise! They could not have retired as individuals, nor met as a body, for such a high purpose without high emotions of some kind. Prayer must have begun well, however it may have been carried on afterward. It seems to have begun when Enos, the son of Seth, was born. Gen. iv. 26: "Then began men to call upon the name of the Lord." Before this time sacrifice seems to have been the chief worship that was practiced or permitted. At least, we have no account of any prayer by Adam, or by any of his family, until the time of Seth; and, therefore, we have no direct warrant to suppose that the privilege of retiring or assembling to pour out the heart freely unto God in prayer was either instituted or allowed, at the same time with the establishment of worship by sacrifice. Permission to "speak unto the Lord," seems to have been a subsequent privilege, wisely withheld until sacrifice paved the way for it, and the death of Abel rendered it a timely and tender mercy to all the shocked and sorrowing household of Adam.

Thus God instituted prayer at first, as he now answers prayer, "in time of need." If this statement surprise you at all, there must be some defect in your estimate of the real grace and grandeur of the privilege of access to God by prayer. You mistake sadly, however, if you imagine that the first men began to pray, as we begin, as a mere act of duty; or if you suppose that they ventured to "make known their wants unto God by supplication and prayer," without a special warrant. They no more offered this "sacrifice of the lips" without express permission, than they offered the sacrifice of the altar without express command. Prayer is as little the dictate of nature or conscience, as sacrifice. Man, left to himself, would neither have prayed nor sacrificed to an invisible God. Consider this matter. It is generally, and justly, allowed, that the idea of worshipping or propitiating God by animal sacrifices is not a dictate of nature. Nothing but the appointment of God could have originated such a practice. Its universality amongst all nations, instead of disproving, confirms this fact. For if the light of nature could not suggest such worship to one nation, it could not lead to it in any nation. Its universality was therefore derived from the force of the original law of Heaven, and upheld by a providence as special as the revelation which introduced that law.

In like manner, the light of nature never led to prayer. Men of all nations have indeed uttered prayers of some kind; and hence it has been almost taken for granted, that prayer is a natural duty, or a kind of human instinct: but it is no more so than sacrifice. Both have been as it were naturalized, in some form, by the force of habit; but both began from the force of divine authority. How could prayer begin otherwise amongst the first men?

Whilst our first parents were in innocence, praise was the only worship in their paradise, as it is in the paradise of heaven. And when they became guilty, they showed by flight and hiding from the presence of God that they had either no desire to pray, or no idea of such a thing. Accordingly, they did not venture to utter a single petition, even when they heard the curse denounced and the promise given. Whatever emotions were awakened by either, no prayerful utterance seems to have been given to them, although God was visibly present. In like manner Cain uttered no prayer when his doom was denounced. See, then, the fallacy of the popular motion, that prayer is natural when misery is pressing. Misery pressed so heavily on Cain, that he said unto the Lord, *"My punishment is greater than I can bear,"* but he seems never even to have dreamt of praying for any mercy or mitigation. Neither did Adam nor Eve (so far as we know), when their sentence was pronounced. Now, if persons in the visible presence of God, and bowed down with wants and woes, never attempted to bow their knees in supplication, how could any man by the light of nature, however laden with fear or grief, dream of praying to the invisible God? If His presence did not suggest the idea, how could his absence teach it apart from revelation? True, there is prayer, where there is no revelation, as we have revelation: but it is all founded in the deathless tradition of the first law of prayer, as all sacrifice is founded on the deathless tradition of the first law of propitiation. I feel in common with you, as if prayer must have always accompanied sacrifice from the very first.

It was so inseparable from sacrifice, from the moment that altars multiplied, until they were all merged in the cross of Christ, that we can hardly believe or conceive that it did not form a part of the very first act of sacrificial worship. There is, however, no positive evidence of its having done so. Abel's offering was, indeed, presented in "faith;" and, that, to us, seems necessarily to include prayer, because it is now almost identified with prayer throughout the Bible: but the question is, was it so from the first? Now we can neither prove that it was, nor show that it must have been so. The object of faith was the promise of a Savior: but however the cordial belief of that promise may have involved an ardent desire for its fulfilment, (and it could not fail to do so, nor operate otherwise) still, that desire neither would nor could break out into prayer, until God revealed Himself as the hearer and answerer of prayer; and we do not know that He did this when he instituted sacrifice. He did it very soon after; but there is no evidence that the appointment of sacrifice and the permission of prayer were simultaneous. But it may be said, what good purpose can be answered by this distinction, however fully it may be established as a fact? I answer, at once—it frees the mind from low and unmanly views of prayer.

Whilst prayer is looked upon as a mere accompaniment of other duties, or merely as a duty, it will neither be loved nor cultivated. It began, however, as a privilege, and it is the highest privilege which God could confer on man, whilst man is out of heaven. The believers in the family of Adam must have felt this deeply when they *"began to call upon the name of the Lord."* They had stood or bowed in utter silence before the altar of burnt-offering, looking, and, no doubt, longing for the day of Christ: and so far, the spirit of prayer was in their sacrificial worship: but it was not until God spoke to them on the subject of prayer that they ventured to speak unto God by prayer. Need I say that their words would be from their hearts when they spoke unto God for the first time! This must have been the case, whether He was visible or invisible, when the first supplications were addressed to Him. If He was visible, there certainly was no irreverence of manner, nor vacancy of spirit, in His presence. The heart could not be "far" from Him, when the lips drew so near to Him: for no man could ramble or mutter over a heartless form of prayer in the immediate presence of Jehovah. If again, God was invisible, *"when men began to call upon"* Him, that invisibility itself would, at first, be a preventive against wandering thoughts and heartless words. It is not so, alas, to us, because we are familiar with it, and have never known anything else, and expect nothing else in this world.

This was not the case, however, with the first men. The invisibility of God must have awed them, much in the same way as His visibility would awe us. The revealed fact He could hear as well in the heaven of heavens, as in Eden or at the altar, both the sigh of penitence and the prayer of faith, must have thrown the whole soul into deep amazement and solemn musing. This must have been a sublime fact, for a long time to all the prayerful. Even the prayer-less must have been struck by the stupendous consideration that no darkness could prevent God from seeing and no distance hinder him from hearing prayer. Not all our familiarity with this sublime fact can so divest the mind of all native simplicity as to prevent amazement, when the fact flashes out upon us vividly.

Look at it now! Who can measure the immensity of space between the footstool on earth and the divine throne in the heaven of heavens? But, only breathe a prayer in the name of Christ, and it is heard by God even whilst you are breathing it. Who can count the intervening myriads of beings and worlds between the spot where you kneel, and the light in which God dwells. You feel lost in the presence of the innumerable multitude; but, only kneel as a suppliant, and the eye of God is as much upon you in in mercy as it is upon angels in love; and the ear of God as open to your cry as to the chorus of glorified spirits. How sublime now is the question, *"Am I God at hand and not a God afar off? Saith the Lord"?* With more than this freshness of realization must the revelation of the hearing of prayer in heaven have struck the men who *"began to call upon the name of the Lord."* They could not have soon contracted an unholy or unfeeling familiarity with the privilege of speaking unto the invisible God. They must long have felt it to be a very solemn exercise. Accordingly, so late as the time of Abraham, we find him prefacing prayer thus, *"Let not the Lord be angry, and I will speak. Behold, now, I have taken upon me to speak unto the Lord, who am but dust and ashes."*

Here, then, is one of the advantages of studying the origin of prayer: we see man and mind in contact with the exercise before forms of devotion were framed, and before native simplicity gave place to artificial tameness or heedless familiarity. Prayer was then what it ought to be still —the simple and sublime act of speaking unto God as a man speaks to his friend; telling Him the secrets, sorrows, and desires of the heart. I do not mean, of course, that the men who began prayer spoke to God with flippancy or without awe of spirit and reverence of manner. Nothing is more disgusting to a well-regulated mind, than the impertinent talk which vulgar minds have invented and called prayer. It is, emphatically, what Solomon calls, "the sacrifice of fools," if not of knaves also. I do, however, mean that prayer began in perfect simplicity, as well as in deep solemnity. Whether uttered as a call, a cry, or a groan, it was direct speaking unto God. He was distinctly realized as looking, and listening, and judging, and feeling, and remembering, all through the act of worship. Prayer was not an exercise of memory, nor an effort of imagination, nor the repetition of a form of words; but just the simple and solemn utterance of the desires of the heart. Men retired alone, or met together, to lay their case for time and eternity before God. They told Him humbly, but freely, all that they felt, and feared, and desired. And whoever will go alone with God to do this will be in no danger of either prating or parading in prayer.

Nothing is so solemn as the childlike utterance of the heart when a man really tries to speak unto God as if God were in the closet listening all the time. It may be well to mention here that the expression in the Hebrews, translated, *"Let us come boldly to the throne of grace,"* is literally, "let us come speaking freely." This wonderful permission simplifies prayer without at all lowering its character or spirit. It relieves the mind from confusion and fear, by confining it to its own immediate wants, and by allowing the utterance of them in its own spontaneous words. It neither forbids the use of forms nor renders them binding; but leaves us perfectly free to adopt either our own expressions or those of others as we feel inclined at the time. And then it confronts us so personally with God that we cannot imagine that we are praying at all (whatever we may be uttering) unless we are consciously and purposely speaking unto God. This view of prayer is not so vividly present to our minds as it deserves to be.

We do well, therefore, to rid ourselves of all artificial and conventional motions of prayer, and to come fairly and fully to the point. It is speaking freely unto God. Have you then "anything to say unto God"? This is the point. You both desire and hope to spend eternity in telling Him how much you owe to His love and mercy by Christ Jesus: and, have you nothing to say now? You are quite sure that when you are in heaven you would at any time quit the company of patriarchs, prophets, apostles, martyrs, even the company of your own family, if you were invited to go up to the eternal throne, to speak freely with God and the Lamb. You would not, for worlds, neglect or decline a single opportunity of speaking "face to face" unto God there. Well; have you nothing to say unto Him here? He will listen to prayer now as readily as to praise then. And you cannot, surely, think that He will admit you to praise there if you dislike prayer here.

Let me persuade you to take this simple view of prayer as retiring to speak unto God at God's special invitation. In this light prayerlessness assumes a very odious aspect, and a very ominous character. How awfully it sounds to say, "there is a man who actually refuses to speak to God!" How ill it looks to be seen trying to avoid all opportunities of speaking unto God. You would not treat a king thus, were he to invite you to an interview at the throne, or in the royal closet. You would not expect a king to repeat his invitations if you had refused even but once. Indeed, there is hardly any man you would refuse to speak to. True, there is a mighty difference between speaking to man, and speaking to God. The difference is, however, all in favor of the latter: for if it be more solemn, it is also infinitely more honorable and useful.

Nothing you could say to the wisest and best of men would procure the pardon of your sins, or a title to heaven, or an interest in the Savior. Were you, indeed, to speak freely about your eternal salvation to a pious and judicious man, his counsel would be of great use, because he would sum it up by encouraging you to pray unto God: and that God Himself calls on and encourages you to do now. Perhaps you rather dislike this repetition of the expression, "speaking unto God." I have said that it simplifies prayer without lessening its majesty or its solemnity; and you feel that, if I be not playing the hypocrite, I am even penetrated with the simple majesty of the idea. Yes; and it has a hold on you, in spite of any objection you feel to it. It will haunt you, even if you try to shake it off tonight, when the hour of prayer comes. Should you then force yourself into bed without prayer, you will be forced to say to yourself, "I am one who refuses to speak to God." And if you try to compromise the matter, by muttering some vague words or heartless petitions, you will almost hear your conscience cry, "this is not speaking to God." Mark and remember my words, and see if the hint does not haunt you.

Here, then, is another good reason for leading you back to the origin of prayer and into the simplicity of its native character. You have heard finer and grander names given to it; but they did not sway you. You could either forget them or get over them, both when you neglected prayer altogether, and when you hurried through it. In fact, "great swelling words" about devotion become plausible excuses for neglecting it. They betray us into the pretense that we are incapable of praying aright yet: but God's call, "come, speaking freely, to the throne of grace," unmasks all this feigned humility by throwing us upon the searching and startling question—"What, have I nothing to say to God?" This is a point not to be got over by either the strength or the stratagem, which vaults over or evades the current forms of the claims of devotion. Try. "Nothing to say unto God—although, through eternity, I expect all my happiness from adoring and serving Him. Nothing to say—although I have sinned against Him, and thus incurred the curse of His law. Nothing to say—although I know not the moment my soul may be required of me! Nothing to say —although, whilst I am spared here, I am entirely dependent on Him for everything?" There it is, you cannot get over this; and it will not be put down.

Oh! If you would ascend to the sublimities of devotion, begin by simply speaking to God. This is the first step on the Bethel ladder of communion with God and the Lamb; and the highest step of the ladder is just "speaking freely," as to a father or a friend; for all the real grandeur of devotion is in the single fact that God is its object, the Lamb its medium, and the Spirit its guide. What we need, therefore, in order to conquer our reluctance, and win our love to prayer, is, just to be fully sensible that we have to speak unto God, and that God will listen complacently whilst we do so.

God listen complacently to us! If you want to have high thoughts of devotion, here they abound. You could not say nor imagine anything higher of the attention which God gave to the first anthem which swelled from the hearts and harps of the angelic morning stars when they began to shine and sing around the eternal throne. All the real glory of any mental exercise of men or angels is just the degree in which God notices and loves it. There would be no moral sublimity in the hallelujah chorus of the skies if God took no pleasure in that high praise. Let His eye be averted from it, or His ear shut to it, or His smile withdrawn from it, and that moment all the golden harps of immortality would be dropped, and all the armies of heaven silent, until some other form of worship was vouchsafed on which God would look with complacency. Now, thus He looks on, and listens to prayer. The seraph's lyre is not more sure of God's attention than the sinner's cry for mercy. Only think before you speak, and then speak into God as you think and feel, and all His heart will be with you.

It is not, however, either so natural or common to think or to speak as we think in prayer as might be expected. When a shrewd diplomatist defined the faculty of speech as the power of concealing our real opinions and designs, he little thought that his political jest implied a solemn religious warning. There is great danger of concealing from ourselves the real state of our hearts, by the language of our prayers, whether that language be our own words, or the words of others. We may not, indeed, intend, nor be exactly conscious of practicing, any imposition upon ourselves, when we pray; and yet our prayers may be complete masks upon the motives and moods of our spirit: for we are quite capable, even before God, both of saying one thing and meaning another, and of saying much and meaning nothing. I do not refer now to attempts to impose on God. It would be worse than useless, at present, to insinuate even a suspicion of your having any tendency to try an experiment so foolish. You have, of course, no more idea that you could deceive omniscience by words than you could defeat omnipotence by strength or stratagem. And you cannot be too firmly "rooted and grounded," in the conviction of the folly of attempting to do either; for both are impossible. We can neither impose upon God, nor force anything against His will.

And as to imposing upon others by your prayers, although that may be attempted, even in the closet, it is too contemptible to be deemed prayer, however it may be practiced. Those who are afraid of being overheard undressing and lying down at night, the moment they retire from the domestic circle; or who are ashamed to have it seen that there could not be a moment for secret prayer in the morning, owing to late rising; may contrive that there shall be a short hush of silence, or a low hum of sound that shall indicate some devotion, and thus keep down suspicion in the family: but all this mean deceit, they feel to be meanly deceitful—as much as the second Charles, when he planned that the puritan ministers who visited him on the continent should overhear him praying in his closet. They did hear him, and were betrayed into a good opinion of him, and were thus led to favor his restoration: but he was not his own dupe. He had too much sense not to despise his hypocrisy, however he plumed himself upon his policy.

And, in like manner, those members of a family who are averse to prayer and yet afraid to betray the full extent of that aversion, do not impose upon themselves by what seems to others the noise of kneeling, and the whisper of devotion. This paltry trick, to evade detection, cannot prevent self-condemnation. It may deceive the parental ear, but it cannot dupe the conscience. It is, however, quite possible to deceive ourselves, both with and without forms of prayer; and that, too, almost unintentionally and unconsciously. Indeed, we actually do so, however regular or reverential our prayers may be, if before and after them, we think nothing about their design or their success. For they are more than acts of worship; there is confession of sin in them, and that is not felt when it is uttered, if it be never thought of in the course of the day. It is not the real sentiment of the heart when it flows from the lips if no sense of the evil of sin flow through the soul at other times. Weigh this fact.

You would not deem it right nor safe to strike out from your prayers the confession that you are a sinner. You could not satisfy yourself without some acknowledgment of your sins. To pass over this point altogether would be so unlike all the inspired specimens of prayer that the contrast would startle you at your own singularity. No wonder. You, therefore, do confess sin when you pray. But, mark if this be neither preceded nor followed by any serious reflection; if your penitence begin and end with your words; if you forget the whole matter until the hour of prayer come round again, your confession of sin is not contrition for sin. Nay; it even hides from you the nature of true repentance. For it is not thus you act, when you have to confess a fault to man. You never did that without both pain and shame. You could not, however you might try to suppress your feelings. I mean by a fault, not, of course, everything which others take offence at; but something which you yourself cannot justify, and you never did condemn yourself, in words, to any man, without both thinking and feeling more than you said. Indeed, what you said was the least part of your repentance, although it may have been the most humiliating. And, is sin against God a lighter matter in your estimation, than an offence against man?

Does confession to the majesty of heaven, who searches the heart, call forth no blush of shame—no tear of sorrow—no throb of pain—no thrill of fear—no forethought nor afterthought? Have you ever been sleepless under the stinging consciousness of a parent's deserved anger, and never felt nor feared the evil of sinning against God but just during the few seconds of time which the confession occupied? If so, your ideas of God are very low indeed! True; He is far more forgiving than man, and far more accessible than offended parties usually are to the offender; but He is not insensible nor indifferent to your sins. They are registered in His books, however the memory or the sense of them may be erased from your conscience. And you are aggravating them all, every time you confess them without forethought and afterthought; for this is adding insult to disobedience.

Accordingly, you would not, you durst not, attempt to settle any serious offence against a human superior, with the cool effrontery of an unfelt and un-weighed apology. You would be afraid of faltering whilst you uttered it, or of being confounded under the glance of a scrutinizing eye. You would not risk the experiment of a hollow or heartless confession before the judges of the land. And yet, you dare to utter words before the Judge of the universe, and words too about your sins against Him, without contrition or consideration.

Perhaps you are now ready to ask, would it them be better not to confess sin at all, than to go through the form of confession, without corresponding feelings? I answer at once—no! I do not think, however, that unfelt confessions are of any use. I am even quite sure that the habit of repeating them, as a matter of course, in prayer, tends to sear the conscience and pervert the judgment. But both conscience and judgment would, in your case, soon sustain more injury if you were to give up confession entirely; because that would be followed by an utter abandonment of all prayer, if not of all the means of grace also; and thus all hold upon you would be lost, until the mighty hand of God laid hold of you by judgments. There is, however, no occasion for giving up the usual habit of confession, nor for confessing without penitence. Remember; the Savior is exalted as a Prince, to "give repentance," as well as "the remission of sin;" and it is as much a part of the office of the Holy Spirit to soften as to sanctify the heart. This pleasing fact should determine you, at once, to rid yourself of all forms of confessing sin (whether they be your own or the phraseology of others) with which you are too familiar, by habit, to be deeply affected. Never mind whose words you give up the use of, if you can use them without thinking, or without feeling that you are speaking to God about your own sins against God. Even an inspired form of confession must be laid aside for a time, if by familiarity it has become a heartless form in your lips.

What God wants and waits to hear from you is not what others have said about sin, but what you think and feel about your own sins. What you have now to consider is whether you have any sentiment, emotion, or conviction of your own on the subject to submit to the ear and to the eye of God. For it is your own opinion of yourself—your deliberate and undisguised judgment of your own heart and character: that is confession of sin. That judgment you must form for yourself by weighing yourself in the balance of the eternal law. Suspend and keep that balance upon the Cross of Christ, by all means; but let divine law be the balance. Yes, your sins have incurred this curse; and it will cleave to your soul if not cancelled by the blood of atonement; and that it will not be, whilst you deem the curse itself too severe.

Now, you do deem the curse of the law too severe. You may not say so; but you think so, and even wonder that any man could judge otherwise. Accordingly, if you were to speak out your real sentiments on the subject of the consequence of sin, you would almost call it unjust; at least, in your own case. You know this to be true, whether you acknowledge it or not. Here, then, is the real cause why you could confess sin, and yet feel little shame or sorrow on account of it: you never believed that it deserved the wrath and curse of God, so far as you were concerned. Did you believe that now, you could not confess yourself a sinner again without both grief and fear. These emotions could not be kept down, were you to allow the conviction of future punishment to spring up in your mind. Confession would rise up from that conviction, like a body emerging from the depths of the sea, wet with tears, or too full of sorrow and shame to weep. Why, then, are you without this conviction?

You have some suspicion that there may be truth in the threatening of hell; for you are afraid to deny it flatly and openly. The Savior himself says so much about "unquenchable fire," and the "impassable gulf" that you dare not maintain the contrary in public, however you may feel in secret. This, also, you know, whether you acknowledge it or not. You neither fully believe, nor fully disbelieve, the Scriptures on this subject. This hesitation will not do! Both confessions of sin, and prayers for pardon, go for nothing at the mercy-seat of God whilst sinners differ from God about the evil and desert of sin. It is only adding insolence to rebellion to ask God to heed or hear an opinion about sin which contradicts His own opinion, or comes short of what He has said. I will not stop to prove that God has said more on this subject than you have believed. I tell you at once the amount of His sentence against sin: it is *"everlasting destruction from the glory of his presence."* Wonder not, therefore, that the Holy Spirit has not helped you to be penitent in confessing sin, nor made you happy in praying for pardon: He could not have done so, without sanctioning your disbelief of God's threatening; and He will never by His work or witness treat God as a liar, whatever you may have ventured to do.

You begin now to see that confession is just to think and speak of your own sins, before God, as God thinks and speaks of them before you in His word. You must agree with Him in opinion about the guilt and danger of sin if you would have Him agree to your petitions for pardon. And as God is not unwilling to accede to your wishes, why should you be reluctant to go all the length in judging of the evil of sin which He has gone in declaring its evil? He is not a man that he should lie or exaggerate. Indeed, the only real wonder in all that God has said of sin and against sin is that His words are not more and stronger; for as nothing but the sacrifice of the incarnate Emmanuel could atone for sin, nothing too strong can be said of the evil of sin. No words can express, no images illustrate, no visions unveil fully the enormity or the malignity of an evil that could only be remedied by the blood of the Lamb.

When "God made his soul an offering for sin," He said all, and infinitely more than all, that words or woes can explain. Away, away, with all quibbling and caviling about the revealed desert of sin: the Lamb of God was slain for it; and He was slain for it because the very principle of sin in the heart (to say nothing of its acts in the life) would have been an eternal barrier—an impassable gulf—between man and heaven. Everlasting banishment from the presence of God, on account of sinfulness, is no arbitrary appointment flowing from abstract law or from absolute will; but the natural consequence of dislike to God and holiness. It is because that dislike is, in itself, an everlasting disqualification or unfitness for heaven, that hell will be the end of all who refuse to be restored to the love of God and holiness. Oh! In understanding be men; for they are childish who talk about hell as too severe. Sin would soon make heaven itself another hell, if "the place prepared," for the unholy might send its inhabitants there, or even if the earth might send the earthly. And were sin less punished or less impaled, there would be no moral security whatever, that the whole universe might not become one hell.

How do you feel disposed to confess sin now I mean your own sinfulness, as a rational, dependent soul, averse to God and godliness? This is your chief guilt and from this is your chief danger of perishing. You quite mistake the matter at issue between God and your soul if you think only of what evil you have done, or if you imagine that all His threatening is mustered against you only for crimes. You are, indeed, criminal before God; and He does not forget this in His threatening. It is however the state of your heart, as alienated from Him as averse to His service and salvation; as fonder of anything than of His will and ways; as having no mature inclination to seek your happiness in His favor and image—it is this state of estrangement from Himself that God looks so closely to and thunders against so loudly. And this inward aversion to give Him your heart has been the real cause of all your guilt and neglect. It is therefore on this point chiefly that your attention should fix and your confession turn, when you retire to speak with God about yourself.

By all means weigh your actions in the balance of the eternal law; you ought and need to see how fearfully they are "wanting;" but, above all, weigh your heart by the weighty claims of supreme love—of perfect confidence—of impartial submission to God; for these are the weights on God's side of the balance. Well, put your heart into the scale on your own side. Ah! It "is lighter than nothing, and vanity." Can you retire now to repeat any man's words before God, or to use your own words in the old way?

Use, by all means, the words which best express your personal convictions and feelings; but make them your own words: vents for the escape of the fullness of your shame and sorrow; helps which unburden your conscience before God. This process will give quite a new turn to your prayers for pardon: hitherto, they have been as superficial as your confessions of sin. In the midst of both you could easily have thought of anything else, and at times you have almost fallen asleep over them. But now you can do neither, unless you can shake off the recollection as well as the impression of these hunting hints; and that you cannot do without doing direct violence to your conscience, and thus deliberately daring God to do His worst.

By this time you begin to anticipate that you shall feel strangely tonight, when you come to bow down before God in prayer; for you cannot speak to Him in your old words unless your new feelings can put all your new meaning into them, and thus make them sound as if you had never uttered nor heard them before. Well; never mind, even if you can find no words to express your feelings: God looketh on the heart, and can both understand and welcome speechless prayer when the spirit is overwhelmed before Him. Think of sin as He thinks—try to fall in with His views of its evil and desert—yield up your whole soul to the mold of his final decisions on the subject; and He will interpret your "expressive silence" as true prayer, until you are able to clothe your desires in corresponding words.

I would have you manfully honest in this matter. Nothing is weaker, meaner, or more unmanly, than the superstitious repetition of unfelt and un-weighed words before the throne of the most high God. There is no virtue, no charm, no use, in any forms of prayer, however ancient or sublime, except so far as they embody and breathe the spirit of our own desires. Good forms may help to kindle these desires and to test their sincerity and strength; but they are not our prayers to God, any farther than they are deliberately and solemnly made so by our own sense of personal danger and our own solicitude for eternal salvation.

6

On Manly Views of Divine Influence

Wherever the gospel is faithfully preached, nothing is more frequently or emphatically insisted upon than the absolute necessity of divine teaching in order to our becoming *"wise unto salvation."* All our best ministers refer us most to "the ministration of the Spirit." Even when their explanations of divine truth are most lucid, and their reasoning most powerful, and their appeal most heart-touching, they disclaim all pretensions to the ability of conveying saving knowledge to our minds, and throw us as fully upon the duty of praying for divine illumination, as if they had done nothing. Indeed, the more they do, in order to explain and enforce the claims of the gospel, the more they confront us with that solemn oracle, *"Not by might nor by power, but by my Spirit, saith the Lord."* Thus, when they most resemble Paul, in their planting, and Apollos in their watering, they most resemble them too, in looking to God for the "increase."

You have noticed this characteristic feature of evangelical preaching. Did it ever surprise you? Perhaps, it has occasionally offended you. Not, of course, that you ever took offence at the modesty of the ministers, who thus ascribed all "the excellency of the power" exclusively to God. Such humility is too beautiful to be offensive. But, have you not, at times, given way to something worse than impatience when you found that the instruction from the pulpit, in order to be useful, must be followed up by prayer in the closet for the teaching of the Holy Spirit." Recollect yourself! Has not dislike to the bare idea of retiring to ponder and pray over an impressive sermon led you into some strange reasoning about the nature and necessity of supernatural teaching? It is not uncommon to evade the claims of secret prayer for the influences of the Spirit, by asking how He teaches, what He teaches, and whether His teaching would not amount to inspiration. When the question is carried thus far, it is then very easy for anyone to smile down the whole matter by saying that he cannot expect to be inspired. This is a very pitiful subterfuge. So is the question, 'what need is there for the work of the Spirit, if the Spirit teach nothing but the truths contained in the Scriptures?' This question may not, indeed, always cloak the base design of getting rid of reflection and prayer: but, like the former, it is very silly and often used for a sinful or slothful purpose. True; the Spirit of God teaches nothing but the lessons contained in the Word of God: but, as they are able to make us wise unto salvation, and as we are naturally averse to learn them, why should the Spirit teach anything else? Nothing else is wanted for the regulation of faith or practice. No man can say, that there is not enough revealed for all holy purposes.

It, therefore, ill becomes those who trifle with what is revealed to complain that nothing more is taught, or to wonder that the Holy Spirit should be the teacher as well as the inspirer of divine truth. It is, indeed, wonderful that He should condescend to follow up His written testimony by his personal agency, and thus "lead into all truth," as well as lay it before us in the Scriptures. He might, and that justly, have thrown us upon our own unaided powers to make the best of the Bible. He has not done so; but, as He pitied our ignorance by furnishing us with a revelation of the character and will of God, so He pities our aversion by promising to take of the things of Christ and "show them" unto us. The necessity of this special teaching is but too obvious from our dislike to learn the will of God. That dislike is so strong that it would defeat all the powers of our mind, even if they were capable of comprehending the full meaning of Scripture, without the help of the Spirit. For, as we naturally dislike what we can comprehend just because it is all so holy and devotional in its character and design, stronger powers of comprehension could only strengthen our natural aversion to practical and humbling truth. Do you not see this? What you do understand of the claims of the gospel, you do not fully approve. You perceive enough upon the very surface of the bible to convince you that it clashes with your inclinations: and, if what you thus see, almost without looking, is disagreeable, because restraining, is it not self-evident, that a perfect understanding of all the holiness of the truth, would increase your hatred to it if your heart remained unchanged.

It is therefore a mercy that our mental powers are not, of themselves, able to grasp the full import of the oracles of God: for, if they could do so whilst our moral tastes continued averse to holiness, knowledge would only exasperate and inflame enmity. Oh, they little know what they complain of, who are displeased when they are told that they cannot become wise unto salvation without divine teaching. The necessity of this is, certainly, a reflection upon the powers of the human mind: but it is also a refuge from the passions of the human heart, which, the more they are crossed, the more craving and clamorous they become. Whilst, therefore, the heart is set upon any sinful indulgence, or averse to moral restraint and devotional feeling, no degree of mental power could elevate the soul to "the love of the truth as it is in Jesus," however far it might raise the soul towards the meaning of that truth.

Besides, there is nothing really strange in fact that nothing but divine power can give divine truth the force of truth upon the human character, or produce the love of it in the human heart. This is, indeed, a melancholy but not at all a surprising, fact. What else could be expected, in a world where all hearts are naturally set against moral restraint, and spiritual exercises: The very arts and sciences would require divine power to teach them effectually, if they involved as much holiness and devotion of the Gospel. Yes; did mathematics demonstrate the evil of sin and the necessity of holiness, just as the cross of Christ does, problems would soon be as unpopular as the doctrines of the cross. Were there no progress could be made in astronomy without as much prayer as watching, there would be but few astronomical students. If geology and botany required, as Mount Zion does, *"clean hands, and a pure heart,"* from all who ascended their hills, neither the strata nor the flowers of the earth would have many visitors. And, if music could never be well played, but when there was *"melody in the heart unto the Lord,"* or when worship was its only object, music, with all its charms, would have but few votaries. Even place and power in the state would not be objects of general ambition if they could only be obtained by spirituality of mind, and only retained by consecration to the glory of God. In a word, were the practical and devotional requisitions of the gospel transferred from the gospel to any trade or science, there would be just as much aversion to that trade or science as there now is to the gospel; and as much necessity for divine influence to enforce their claims.

For it is not the mystery of a revelation from Heaven, nor the mysteriousness of what is revealed, but the design of it all that is offensive to human nature. We are naturally fond of the mysterious when it does not interfere with our comfort; and, therefore, it is only a pretense to mask disinclination when mystery is pleaded as an excuse for unbelief, or indecision. It is "a lion," only in those ways which men dislike to walk in. Thus it is not so much the weakness of our natural faculties as it is the worldliness and carnality of our affections that renders the Work of the Holy Spirit indispensable. It is, therefore, almost a useless, if not also a foolish question, to ask, how much a man could learn from the study of the Scriptures, without any divine teaching! For, what if he could acquire, by dint of application, the true meaning of all the bible: it could not benefit his soul, so long as his heart hated what his understanding comprehended. No knowledge of heavenly things could overthrow the supremacy of earthly things in a mind that preferred earthly things. Great knowledge might counterbalance, a little, his worldliness, by embittering some of his enjoyments, and embarrassing some of his movements; but it could not change his heart, whilst he was unwilling to exchange an earthly for a heavenly portion.

The real form of the question ought, therefore, to be, how much will a man learn of truths which reprove and pain him, and which he therefore dislikes? And you can answer this question from your own experience. Like yourself, he will not try to learn much, except when some fear of perishing prompts him to search the Scriptures. In thus disposing of this question, I do not forget that masterly defenses of Christianity have been written by men who never prayed for the illuminations of the Holy Spirit. Some, even by men who did not believe that there was such a Spirit. These works are, therefore, proofs of what can be done without His teaching. They are, however, easily accounted for by the premiums of fame or rank which, in a Christian country, await the triumphs of talent and learning. There is no aversion in the human mind to write down a rival system, nor to write up an endowed system. That study of the Scriptures which qualifies a man for such public controversy does not involve secret devotion nor a supreme desire to glorify God. It can begin in ambition, and go on in pride; and, at last, leave the writer more earthly-minded than it found him. It is, therefore, only another proof of the necessity of divine teaching, in order to our becoming *"wise unto salvation."*

We may, without the Spirit, become wise unto fame, or wise unto wealth, or wise unto victory, in polemical questions of great public interest; but wise unto salvation we cannot become apart from the agency of the Holy Spirit, because neither talent nor study can, by themselves, produce love to God, or conformity to the image of Christ. And, what is any degree of religious knowledge worth to its possessor, if it leave him estranged from the love and kindness of God and the Lamb? Remember; it is principles you need: and they cannot be acquired apart from the influences of the Spirit. Notions may be acquired without His help; but they can do little for you in time and nothing for you through eternity. Accordingly, what benefit have you derived from the vague knowledge you possess of the gospel? You are not utterly ignorant of it, nor altogether indifferent about it; and yet, its promises do not gladden your heart, nor its principles regulate your life, nor its glorious prospects soften the aspect of death, or brighten the aspect of eternity. Thus, it is, in fact, no gospel to you, as yet. It might, indeed, be mere law, for any comfort you obtain from it. It is, however, "glad tidings of great joy;" and this is the knowledge of it which the Spirit teaches. This is what you have not learned; and what you cannot learn without being "taught of God."

Consider this fact. You quite mistake, if you imagine that the gospel has no other design upon you than to restrain and regulate your character. It has that design upon both your heart and life: but it has also an express regard to your happiness. Yes; to your immediate as well as your eternal happiness. To say that you are not happy, I do not mean that you have no enjoyments: I mean that you cannot enjoy yourself when you think of God. You are obliged to forget Him whenever you try to enjoy yourself; and that, not only when you seek happiness in the pleasures of sin, but also when your pleasures are both rational and harmless. Even then, you are glad to keep clear of all recollections of God, lest they should spoil your enjoyment. And, as to recollections of eternal things, they actually embitter the sweetest cup of your pleasure, whenever they intrude themselves. And, call you this happiness? Can you think, even for another moment, that you understand the Gospel, or that you can understand it without the Spirit, whilst you regard the God of love in this light! What a perversion of language, to call that enjoyment, which can be spoiled and dispersed by recollections of the glory and grace of Jehovah! It is such another contradiction in terms as saying that the sun spoils a landscape, or that the moon disfigures a sea-view. I tell you again—you do not understand the gospel: for God, as it reveals Him, may be recollected with joy, in connection with every pleasure and pursuit which is not criminal: and realized, without pain or embarrassment, in every scene and circle which is not vicious.

He that loveth not God *"knoweth not God, for God is love."* Away with the low and unmanly notion that God is merely a jealous spy, or a harsh judge, upon human happiness. He grudges no enjoyment but what is sinful, and frowns on no pleasure but that which displaces Him in the heart, and thus perils the soul. His supreme object is to glorify Himself by promoting our happiness. Do not say, in answer to this—"that is, if we seek our happiness in meditation, and in prayer, and in doing good, God will promote it." That is not all; nor is it a fair representation of the fact which it professes to describe. Meditation, and prayer, and obedience, are not exactly what they now seem to you. You are judging of them as mere abstract and absolute duties, which trench on time and clash with convenience. You are looking at them only in their connection with this life, and overlooking their connection with eternal life. This is not fair. I do not mean that the light of eternity, as you now view eternity, would materially alter your opinion of duty or devotion. You do not understand the gospel sufficiently yet, to look it fully in the face. It is to you, as yet, what God seems to you, an object of dread rather than of admiration. How, indeed, could either be otherwise, for all the heed you have given to them?

But, to the point, I defy you to make out even to yourself, anything like a proof that the glad tidings of the gospel as they are found in the Bible could not make you happy now. You may make out a case against devotion, which, in the present state of your mind would convince you that prayer and watchfulness could not be pleasant. But were you an infidel, or even an atheist, I would openly and calmly defy you to prove the glorious gospel to be unpleasant. For, could it be proved to be untrue (which it cannot), even that would not alter nor affect the truth of the grand principle on which it rests. Be not surprised at this assertion. Nothing can disprove that eternal happiness would be an infinite blessing. The truth of this does not depend on the truth of anything else. This would be true even if there were not a soul in man, nor a God in the universe. There could not in that case be, of course, eternal happiness in point of fact; but in point of theory, it would remain incontrovertibly true that eternal happiness would be an infinite blessing. Now, it is upon this independent fact, which no man in his senses can either deny or doubt, that the gospel founds its claims upon the attention and love of all men.

The gospel argues with no man about his likes or dislikes of duty and devotion, until it has offered him a boon which he cannot dislike, however he may try: for it is absolutely impossible, even to find fault with eternal happiness. So it is—to be reconciled to the sad end of those who disbelieve. Both may be disbelieved or forgotten: but neither can be despised. God has taken care to render that impossible. Accordingly, it is not heaven itself, but the way to it, that you dislike. It is not hell itself, that you care nothing about, when you are careless of your soul. It is not, therefore, the gospel in its final results, that you can make out a case against, but the gospel in its initiatory and intermediate demands. You can no more hate heaven than you can love hell, however much you may hate the narrow way which leads to everlasting happiness. Here, then, is the point at which the gospel itself meets you, with its practical and devotional claims. God is fully aware that you do not love them, nor see how they would conduce to your happiness. He wants you, however, to love them; and, therefore, He presents to your view and offers to your acceptance what you cannot dislike, even if you were to set yourself with all your might to try to dislike it; for it is nothing else, and nothing less, than certain escape from the wrath to come, and eternal happiness in the presence, favor, and image of God and the Lamb, in company with all the unfallen and restored spiritsf in the universe.

Now it is prayer, as it secures this portion; watchfulness, as it fits for this inheritance; duty, as it prepares for this society, that the gospel urges and enforces: and when the claims of eternity are fairly weighed, the claims of duty and devotion will be fairly met. The latter cannot be evaded when the former are duly and daily considered.

What think you now of the necessity of the work of the Spirit? Can anything but Divine power bring eternity so home to your habitual consciousness that aversion to duty must fall before its presence? Do you not see and feel that both the first and the final appeals of the gospel are founded upon invisible realities, which can only be vividly realized with delight by a mind divinely aided and influenced In a word? Look at the whole mass of your natural and acquired distaste for eternal things; and then at the utter improbability of its giving way of its own accord; and then at the absolute necessity of its overthrow, before you can love divine things; and say, is it not an infinite mercy that the help of the Holy Spirit is promised in answer to prayer, and in connection with searching the Scriptures? Who would not place himself under such a teacher as "the Spirit of wisdom and revelation"? Sitting at His feet, to become wise unto salvation, is almost as sublime and quite as useful as meeting Him on the mount of vision was, when prophets were His scholars, and prophecies His lessons.

Perhaps it may now be well, before entering upon the still more special work of the Holy Spirit on the heart, to prove to you the reality of His teaching. I mean, that He does teach now. You remember the promise, *"they shall all be taught of God."* Well; be not surprised when I say that this promise is literally fulfilled, in the case of all true believers. They may seem to you, at first sight, to have learned very different lessons; for they are certainly very much divided in sentiment amongst themselves. Hence arises the question, how can they all be taught of God? He surely does not teach one to be a Calvinist, and another to be an Armenian; nor one to be a Churchman, and another to be a Dissenter. And yet, the pious of both parties are taught by the Spirit. How is this? Look, first, at the grand points in which they all fully agree. All the truly pious are of *"one heart and one mind,"* as to the way and the design of salvation, by grace. They all unite in perfect harmony around the cross, and before the mercy-seat. Now, what could produce this union of sentiment and feeling, but Divine teaching? What better proof could be given, that they have all been in one school, and under one master? For, remember; this agreement in the new song is not confined to one nation; but in every nation all who really believe in Christ believe the same things concerning Christ, and for the same purpose, too. And now, as to what they differ about, the fact is, there has been no Divine teaching on either side, when the Scriptures have not been allowed to speak for themselves. The Spirit leads only into all revealed truth.

Personal religion is, however, my subject. Now, when the Scriptures affirm the absolute necessity of *"a new heart,"* and call the change *"regeneration,"* they do not speak in the language of the world, nor according to the natural opinions of mankind; and yet, they forbid us to reckon the doctrine of the new birth strange. *"Marvel not that I say unto you, ye must be born again."* The Savior expressed surprise, as well as censure, when Nicodemus attempted to mystify the subject, and thus to evade its claims: *"art thou a master in Israel, and knowest not these things?"* That there is mystery in the mode of divine operations on the human mind, the Savior not only did not deny, but also asserted it in unqualified terms: *"the wind bloweth where it listeth, and thou hearest the sound thereof, but canst not tell whence it cometh, or whither it goeth: so is every one that is born of the Spirit."* After these explicit assurances from the lips of Him who is both our Savior and our Judge, it would be equally unmanly to overlook the mystery, or to dispute the necessity of a divine change on the heart. Both are asserted by the same high authority; and therefore ought to be treated with the same holy reverence. This is not done, however, when the declared mystery of the mode of spiritual operation is turned into an excuse for neglecting to pray for *"the renewing of the Holy Ghost."* That *"washing of regeneration"* ought to be prayed for with as much simplicity of heart as when we ask for our daily bread, and with infinitely more solicitude. There is mystery in the way in which our food nourishes our natural life: but, whoever rejected or neglected food, because he could not explain the process by which it sustains the body? It prolongs life and renews strength; and, therefore, every same man uses it, and every good man prays for it. In like manner, it is the fact that the Word of God, when duly weighed and prayed over, is blessed by the Spirit of God, to the renovation of the soul. No man ever imitated David, in hiding the Word of God in his heart, and in praying for a new heart, without finding in his own experience the truth of the promise, *"A new heart will I give you, and a new spirit will I put within you: and I will take away the stony heart out of your flesh, and give you a heart of flesh. And I will put my Spirit within you, and cause you to walk in my statutes."*

I have already stated, that we are solemnly warned against marveling at the necessity of a change of heart. And no man can look at heaven, in the purity of its enjoyments, or in the spirituality of its engagements, and *"marvel,"* that he must be *"born again,"* in order to enter the kingdom of heaven. This is no more a wonder, than that an ignorant man is unfit to fill the chair of Newton, or a weak man to guide the helm of a free nation. Both the place and the pleasures of eternal life render the renewal of the soul as necessary, as they render the resurrection change of the body indispensable. *"Flesh and blood cannot inherit the kingdom of God."* Accordingly, no one marvels, that this mortal body *"must put on immortality,"* before it can take its place in heaven. We both admit and admire the necessity of having this "vile body" changed and fashioned, into the likeness of "Christ's glorious body." We feel, instinctively, that its present weakness, and especially its grossness are incompatible with *"an exceeding and eternal weight of glory."*

And, is not a corrupted soul as unfit for heaven, as a corruptible body? If the latter must "bear the image of the heavenly," surely the former cannot do without it. Marvel not that ye must be born again in order to inherit the kingdom of God! You yourself feel that if your body were to rise from the grave unchanged, your soul, if holy, would shrink back from all reunion with it, and prefer to be "unclothed" forever, rather than to be again imprisoned in such a clay tabernacle: and I tell you plainly, that were your body to rise from the dead, *"fashioned like unto Christ's glorious body,"* it would, as instinctively, shrink back from reunion with your soul, if your soul were unholy. Wonder not, therefore, that both must undergo a divine change, before they can enter heaven.

A matter which can thus be brought home to our common sense is not likely to be without analogies in our common nature. You may not have noticed yet, with an express reference to this subject, how much the heart can be changed for a time, by the mere force of circumstances. There are, however, both moods and emotions, common to man, which prove that the heart may be brought into a full harmony with the mind and will of God. Many providential events bring men to the very brink of acquiescence, in all that God requires; and, were the feeling of the moment followed up by consideration and prayer, full acquiescence would be the effect of these dispensations. Have you ever lost, by death, a beloved parent, brother, or sister? Remember the state of your heart, whilst stunned or melted by that bereavement. You had no occasion to try experiments, nor to take measures, in order to feel as the rest of the family felt. The loss affected you at the same time, and in the same way, that it did others. Your spirits sank—your heart melted—your whole soul quivered with deep emotion. You may have wept less than some of the family did; but you did not feel less, when you gazed the last look upon the face you were to see no more, *"until the heavens and the earth were no more."* You had your full share in all the real suffering which pervaded the domestic circle, when you first met that circle, after the final interview in the chamber of death. Every convulsive shriek and sob, during that solemn meeting, went to your heart. For the time, all worldly recollections passed away from your mind. You could not have planned nor executed any earthly enterprise, however gainful or tempting. Whatever was the absorbing subject of public attention, at the moment, you were almost insensible to its very existence; and too much absorbed at home to have any personal sympathy with it. Your thoughts and feelings were concentrated upon the breach—the blank—made in the family circle. Remember also, how attentively you listened to the chapters of the Word of God, which were read that evening. They were full of meaning, and almost sounded as if you never read them before. You felt no inclination to quarrel or cavil with the oracles of God. You were glad to find, that there was so much in them suited to the house of mourning, and to the bleeding heart. Even prayer, however you may have felt it to be "a weariness" before or since, was then soothing. You joined in it instinctively, and enjoyed it much, when it placed you under the pitying eye and the shadowing wing of a paternal God. Even when it led your thoughts direct to "the blood of the Lamb," as the only plea for pardon; and to the grace of the Holy Spirit, as the only source of purity, you fell in with the strain of the petitions, and were not unwilling to be an entire debtor to the mercy of the Cross.

You saw so clearly—and felt so keenly—how life, and health, and reason, depend on the will and power of God, that you could neither doubt nor wonder that salvation should depend upon His goodwill. In a word, you were *"almost persuaded to be a Christian,"* whilst the infinite importance of being "altogether" a Christian, lay before you in the strong light of death, judgment, and eternity. Thus God *"maketh the heart soft,"* in the day of bereaving visitation. In such a scene, even Hume burst into tears, and exclaimed, "O that I had never doubted." Now, although all this does not amount to a spiritual change of heart, it was a moral change, which, while it lasted, corresponded with the providential dealings of God with your family: and still it is both proof and illustration to you of the possibility of having your heart brought as fully under the power of the Word of God, by His Spirit, as it was then under the power of His rod, by His providence. For, if such be the force of circumstances, when they are solemn and painful, what may not the force of eternal truth effect on the heart, when accompanied by the gracious influences of the eternal Spirit? This is the point on which I would now concentrate your attention.

Add, if you will, to their tender and intense emotions I have just recalled, all the deep emotions you have ever experienced. You have been very ill at times; and your heart was softened then. You have had some signal escapes from imminent danger; and your heart melted then. You have witnessed scenes of woe and suffering; and your sympathies overcame you. You have even been dissolved in tears, by reading a tale of deep interest; and, amidst the solitudes of nature or the grave, you have mused, until your spirit was in full communion with all the aspects and associations of the scenery. Well; to all these fine emotions, I make my appeal. You justly regard them as manifestations of good taste and right feeling; and thus as proofs that you are not heartless nor frivolous. So do I. Such sympathies and sensibilities identify you with all who can think and feel. No mind can reach manhood without them. I appeal, however, to what you have felt under the pressure of affliction, or in the presence of suffering, or amidst the silence and solitude of impressive scenes, in order to show you what you may feel and ought to feel, under the disclosures and overtures of eternal life.

Now you would be ashamed of yourself if you had not wept when the family grave was open—if you had not softened when the mighty hand of God brought you low—if you had not yearned with sympathy when real and heart-rending suffering fell under your notice. And, is it no shame to be unmoved by the curse of a broken law? No shame to be un-melted by the atoning sufferings of the Son of God? No shame to be heedless about that "holiness, without which no man shall see the Lord? Judge righteous judgment; I will not call your sensibility vapid sentimentalism; nor your sorrows selfish because they terminate upon earthly things; but I will, I must say, that it is as unmanly as it is ungodly to be unfeeling whilst your soul is in peril, and your eternal all in jeopardy. This admits of no apology or palliation. It is equally weak and wicked: as intellectually mean as it is morally base. You, yourself, despise this heartlessness, and denounce such heedlessness when they trifle with temporal interests, or with human sorrows. You could not think well of any man, whatever were his rank in science or society who could treat his lowest friend as you have treated your God and Savior.

I refer now, not to your sins, nor to your short-comings; but to the sheer trifling with salvation, which you have indulged. Your soul might need neither mercy nor grace, from the way you have treated it; or mercy and grace might never have cost the Savior a tear nor a groan, from the way you have treated them. This will not do. You must be born again. All the character of God and heaven must change for the worse if you could be safe for eternity without a change to the better. You as much need a new heart now as you will need an immortal body at the resurrection. And you are not the person, whoever may be so, to shelter yourself under the question of Nicodemus, *"How can these things be?"* The spiritual change you need can be just as the moral changes I have mentioned have been. You can neither deny nor doubt the power of Providence to soften your heart; and, therefore, you cannot question the power of grace, to sanctify it. You have been moved—melted—penetrated, by what God has done; and as He has said greater things in His Word than any He has done by His rod, greater impressions and improvements may, under the blessing of His Spirit, be produced by them, on your heart and character. Thus, there is no mystery to you, in the necessity of a new heart and a right spirit; for, by your own acknowledgment, you have already experienced that change of tone and temper, which circumstances can produce: and that, although not regeneration, is quite enough to prove that the heart can be regenerated; and more than enough to explain how it may be so.

Let there be, therefore, no equivocation or evasion, on this point. I tell you again, that God "hath made your heart soft," by means, with which the agency of His Spirit is not necessarily connected, nor directly promised: and, if they could bring you "to your right mind" for a time, what may not the special means of grace (with which the work and witness of the Holy Spirit are connected by covenant) do for you, and in you? For, if the coffin and the grave of a parent, a relative, or a friend, have, without any reference to the agency or the existence of the Spirit, thrown you into such moods of thought and feeling, that, whilst they lasted, the world was a blank—business a burden—and the bare idea of amusement hateful, what might not the study of the cross and tomb of the Savior effect, were that study carried into the closet, and conducted with an express reference to "the mighty working" of the Eternal Spirit? Do not evade the point of these questions by asking, whether the renewing work of the Spirit, like the softening work of Providence, renders "the world a blank—business a burden—and amusement hateful?" You know that it does not.

My design can only be mistaken willfully; can only be misrepresented wantonly. Nothing is further from it (and the inmost voice of your conscience tells you so), than to convey an idea that you must be thrown, by the work of the Spirit, into the same agitation, or into the same depression, or into the same deadness to the world, which you felt during the paroxysms of pain or grief. It is not for this end the Spirit of God works; not in this way that His influences operate. I mean, it is not to produce a continuance of painful emotions, or low spirits, that he awakens the conscience, and melts the heart. He does wound; but it is that He may heal. He does humble; but it is, that He may revive and cheer "the contrite ones." There is nothing in His work on the heart to prevent the due discharge of social duties, or the due enjoyment of social life; but, as the healing hand of time leads bereaved mourners gently and gradually back to their wanted composure and proper business, without doing any violence to the sacredness of their sorrows; so the Spirit of all grace leads back the penitent mourner, to his proper place and work in society, under the influence of hopes and principles which qualify him to do well for both worlds. There is, in conversion, sorrow for sin; but there is also the hope of pardon; and, what honest or rational pursuit could be hindered by either?

There is, in conversion, self-abasement before God; but there is also love to God, and some reliance on Him: and what laudable enterprise or virtuous enjoyment could these spoil or prevent? There is, in conversion, a spirit of prayer and watchfulness; but there is also a spirit of dependence on Grace and Providence, and, that must be a very questionable business, and that a more equivocal pleasure, which would be injured by either spirit.

Marvel not that ye must be born again; for there is nothing in the change to turn activity into idleness, or cheerfulness into melancholy, or energy into weakness, or manliness into pusillanimity. All the proper business of life would be better conducted; all the real enjoyments of life more relished; all the noble pursuits of life more successful, and all the poetry of life more lovely, were they combined with the vital godliness of a regenerated heart. Cowper did not cease to be a poet when he became "altogether a Christian." The harp of Montgomery rose in sublimity, in proportion as his heart ascended by the cross, to the throne. Would there were no necessity for such remarks I feel ashamed of making them. Not, of course, that I doubt their truth at all; nor that I care little for the genius which has been allied with piety: but I am ashamed to plead the claims of the Eternal Spirit, by proving that they do not clash with public duty or mental improvement. Oh, there ought to be no necessity for demonstrating or illustrating this fact, by appeals to the living or to the dead.

The mighty God, the Lord, hath spoken, and said, *"ye must be born again;"* and the splendor of all the thrones and crowns of glory attests it; the letter and spirit of all the songs of heaven repeat it; the eternal harmony and communion of saints and angels imply it; and every manly, as well as revealed, idea of fellowship with God and the Lamb, suggests and confirms the universal necessity of "a new heart." I know not, of course, the precise circumstances under which you read these hints. You may have stood, lately, by the death-bed and the grave of an endeared parent or friend; and if so, you were not unmoved by the scene. You have not forgotten it; and you feel as if you never could forget it: it was so solemn and affecting. Well, it is not the emotions of that trying moment I want to revive. I have no wish to re-open your wounds, nor to renew that sense of desolation which then awed and agitated your soul. I just refer to them—that I may refer you to an experimental proof of the fact that the heart can be changed in its tone and temper by the power of solemn providences: and if they, by their own impressiveness, could give quite a new cast to your spirit for a time, you thus see (and cannot wonder when you see it), how the solemn realities of salvation and eternity, may become the means of a divine and permanent change of heart and character. Your emotions have corresponded with the dispensations of Providence; and, in the day of calamity, you would have reckoned yourself fool-hardy or unfeeling, if you had not stood in awe of the hand of God.

Now, what is wanted, in order to your being *"a new creature in Christ Jesus,"* is, just that your views and feelings should correspond with *"the truth as it is in Jesus;"* or, that what God has said and sworn in the Gospel, should make its own impression on you, just as what He has done has made its own impression on you. And, why should not His Word be as influential and effective as His rod? Mark and weigh, then, the facts of your own case. You are not a stranger to the softening of heart, which the subduing hand of Providence can produce. You now see, that if the Gospel were brought home to your feelings, as pain and loss have been, you must yield to its influence. Well; the mighty hand of God touched you, just that you might thus know by experience that your heart was susceptible of a saving change; and, that you might follow up the emotions of a common change, by prayer for the quickening and converting influences of the Holy Spirit. O, believe God, when He says, that He *"worketh all these things, in order to save souls alive."* He has not been your enemy, nor unkind to you, in thus making you to drink of the cup of sorrow so soon. He put it into your hand, for the express purpose of drawing your attention to *"the cup of salvation."* He made the former bitter, that the latter might be sweet. You were overlooking *"the water of life;"* or refusing it; or flattering yourself that you would drink in time enough, if you drank before you died. God marked this; and, in mercy, gave you a check! He loved your soul too well to spare your feelings: for He meant you good, and not evil, when He made you feel through all your soul, that all your comforts could be crushed in a moment. This was, indeed, a severe lesson, but a salutary one, and intended to prevent the severer lessons of judicial wrath. Whereas, God dealeth with you as with sons; *"for what son is he whom the father chasteneth not?"*

Oh, I would not for worlds entertain the vague motions of suffering or sorrow, which are afloat, even amongst those who talk about "some wise and good end, to be answered by our trials." There is such an end intended by God: but it is both wiser and better than anything which is usually meant by this familiar phrase. All that it amounts to in popular opinion, is, that trials may be a paving the way for brighter days; and, in the meantime, improving the general character of the sufferer. Now, although there be much truth in this interpretation, the grand truth is not distinctly in it. That is—that trials form one of God's methods of saving "souls alive," by leading sufferers and mourners direct to the cross and the mercy-seat, to seek for grace. Salvation is the end which God has in view, by the discipline of Providence. The good He intends, is a definite, an infinite, an eternal blessing. It embraces, indeed, the general improvement of the character: but it bases and begins that renewing of the heart, by leading out the soul to the glories of the atonement; by bringing the conscience and the understanding under the authority of truth, and of the Spirit of truth and holiness. Mark my words. God sympathizes with your sorrows, far more than any of those who weep whilst you weep. I do not mean that your friends are insincere in their sympathy: but I do mean that they cannot hold your sorrows so sacred as God does. He sees in them, and intends by them, that, which may lead you safe into the heaven of heavens, by leading you direct to the hope set before you in the Gospel. Now, His design you must fall in with, if you would get real good from your trials. All their natural influence, however moral in its character for a time, will be as the early cloud and the morning dew, evanescent.

Many have wept at the family grave who are now laughing in the chair of the scorner or the drunkard. Many, who imagined that they had buried their vices and their vanity in the parental tomb, are now filling up the measure of their iniquity, and taking their swing in both crime and folly. If, therefore, you meant well, by any promise you gave to a dying mother; by any tear you shed at a father's sepulcher; by any pledge you gave to the God of heaven, when He made your heart soft, follow up, follow out your resolutions—by following Providence to the cross of Christ. Providence arose to lead you there. To bring you there—it smote you. To drive you there—it repeated its strokes. And the explanation of all its discipline is this, *"What is a man profited, if he gain the whole world and lose his own soul?"* Lose it he must, unless he set himself by consideration and prayer to invite and invoke the renewing influences of the Holy Ghost.

Let no man deceive you on this subject. Tell every man who makes light of a divine change that he cannot resist the change which Providence brings on the spirits, when health gives way, or losses set in, or bereavements create desolation at home. Why should it be thought a strange thing, that the heart should be sanctified by a God, who so often softens it!

7

On Manly Views of Religious Mystery

If the man who first said that, "Religion ends where mystery begins," imagined that he had uttered a smart thing, he must have been weaker than the witlings who repeat it. The terseness of the antithesis led them to adopt it as a maxim. It tickled their ear, and thus betrayed their judgment. They were misled by taking for granted that what was so well expressed must be well founded. No such excuse, however, can be put forward, on behalf of the author of this sounding fallacy. It duped him before it acquired its witty form. The eyes of his understanding were hoodwinked, before his ear was tickled: unless, indeed, he was more traitor than fool. But however this may be, no man, whose sense and sincerity are equal, could be misled, for a moment, by such a statement. It is as false and absurd as to say, that "travelling ends where the sea begins." The mode and the medium of travelling end where the sea begins; but the motion goes on, in the new element, as well as on land. In like manner, religion need not end where mystery begins. There is "a path in the dark waters" of mystery, as well as on the table-land of morality. Adoration, modesty, and faith may go on wisely, even when comprehension must stop, and reason hesitate.

"*We walk by faith, not by sight,*" says Paul; and in saying this, in regard to religion, the apostle said no more than every man does, in almost all the affairs of ordinary life. Both life, and the means of life, are full of mystery, and call for as much implicit faith, as the great mystery of godliness requires. For what aliment of our subsistence do we comprehend, either in its original elements, or in its adaptation to our nourishment mankind have, in fact, nothing to go by, in the use of food, but faith and experience. I say, faith—as well as experience: for no length of experience, as to the usefulness of any article of home or foreign consumption, could prove to a certainty, that the new supply is as nutritious as the old stock. Thus we are thrown, from year to year, on the principle of implicit faith, in God and man — in God, by believing that he has not altered the qualities of the crops; and in man, by believing that neither the growers, nor the sellers of provision have poisoned it. Thus we actually live, by faith in the constancy of Providence, and in the general integrity and humanity of mankind. Without implicit faith in both, we should be haunted with the suspicion of poison, whenever we eat or drink. And, were any man to reject food, until he could understand and explain the entire nature of liquids and solids, who does not see that he must starve?

Thus there would be no more folly in saying, "that eating should end where mystery in food begins," than there is in saying that religion ends where mystery begins. It is just as truly ascertained by experience, that religion, with all its mysteries, does good to all who meekly believe them; as it is, that food, with all its mysteries, sustains those who use it. Indeed, if mystery ought to stop or disturb anything in the affairs of life or godliness, what would it not put an end to; for they are all based on mysteries.

Were religion to end where mystery begins, religion could not begin at all, in earth or heaven. For, were religion nothing but mere "bodily service," in obedience to simple rules, the very utterance of these rules by God, and the bare apprehension of them by man, would be inexplicable mysteries. Our familiarity with the power of words to convey ideas renders us insensible to this fact: but, the moment we try to explain or comprehend that power, we are lost. It is as much a mystery as instinct. In a word; a religion without mystery, must be a religion without a God: for the moment a God is admitted, mystery begins, and can never end. Unitarianism pretends, indeed, to be a religion without mysteries: and, certainly, it is not the fault of its votaries, that any mystery cleaves to that system. They have done all that men could do to rid it of them; and somewhat more than even the devil ever ventured to try; for he did not venture to question the inspiration of the texts quoted against his proposals in the wilderness, nor to evade their force by analyzing their figures. But still, after all that has been dared and done, to rid Unitarianism of mystery, even the oneness of its God leaves him incomprehensible : and, what more, can Trinitarianism make Him? I readily allow that there is less mystery in the theory of one person in the Godhead, than in the revelation of three persons in the unity of the Godhead: but, as even the Unitarian theory ascribes infinity or omnipresence to its God, it thus announces so much mystery, that the faith which bows to that infinity need not stagger at the revealed plurality of the divine essence. That essence may surely subsist in inconceivable forms, seeing it is allowed, even by simplifiers, to pervade the infinitude of space. This is, however, a question of pure revelation; and, therefore, may be soon settled. I say "soon," because there cannot be "two sides" of the question in the Bible. For, if it be the fact that there is but one person in the Godhead, it is also the fact, that the Bible is intended to teach the unity of the Godhead; and, therefore, all that the Bible says must be on one side of the question. There is either nothing in it about the Father alone being God, or all that is in it ascribes divinity to no one else. But what is the fact? It is, that the lively oracles proclaim the divinity of the Son, as much as the divinity of the Father; and claim for Him all the works and worship which they ascribe to the Father. And, is this the way to teach, that there is but one person in the Godhead? This is the way in which revelation teaches the unity of the Godhead.

In like manner, it ascribes to the Holy Spirit, both the attributes and operations which are peculiar to Deity. Accordingly, on almost all minds, in all nations to whom "the word of God has come," it has left the impression that there is a Trinity in the Godhead. Even on the minds of those who deny the Trinity, the Bible has left a conviction, that it requires much learning, labor, and dexterity, to prevent it from making men Trinitarians. It keeps Unitarians forever on the stretch, to counteract its natural influence on the public mind. Weigh these facts. Had the Bible been intended to teach mankind that the Father alone is God, there would have been nothing in it contrary to this; nothing inconsistent with this; nothing to cloud or encumber this; yea, there ought to have been nothing in it, that could suggest the bare idea of the Son or the Spirit being divine also : but there is so much in it contrary to, and inconsistent with, the exclusive divinity of the Father, that almost all who receive the Scriptures as a revelation from heaven become Trinitarians; and even those who do not become so can only maintain their existence as a sect, by expunging many parts of the Bible, and explaining away the obvious sense of more.

Now, no Unitarian book produces any such impression upon the mind of its readers. Neither criticism nor caution is needed, in order to prevent us from imagining that Priestley or Belsham taught the doctrine of the Trinity. Both the letter and spirit of their writings are uniformly and unequivocally against it. Why, then, is not the Bible equally against the Trinity, if the doctrine be untrue! Why is there anything in Scripture that suggests the bare idea of three persons in the Godhead, if there be only one? No other rational answer can be given to these questions than that the Bible never was intended to teach the exclusive divinity of the Father. Accordingly, it has led the immense majority of all who have read it to believe that Father, Son, and Spirit, are one Jehovah. There is, indeed, mystery in the doctrine of the Trinity: but both the Bible and Providence would be a "mystery of iniquity," if it were not true; for they spread widely, and support uniformly, nothing else, on the subject of the divine nature. If, therefore, there be great mystery in the doctrine, all the great miracles of omnipotence, and all the great measures of Providence, and all the signal monuments of antiquity, and all the populous traditions of the world, are on its side. It is not an unsanctioned nor an un-enshrined mystery. The seal of heaven accredits its truth, and the smiles of heaven accelerate its triumphs. Amidst the number and splendor of its vouchers and victories, it is almost impossible to remember that there is, or ever was, in existence, such a petty thing as Unitarianism. It is, therefore, more than mystery, that he rejects, who rejects the Trinity. In doing that, he sets himself in opposition to all the verdicts of experience, and to all the visions of immortality: for the former accredit no other gospel but the Trinitarian, as *"the power of God unto salvation,"* or even unto moral reformation; and the latter illustrate nothing more clearly, than that all the armies of heaven unite in *"honoring the Son, even as they honor the Father."*

Look at the latter fact first. You know nothing of heaven, but just what is revealed concerning it. No man has any more information on the subject, or can obtain more. It is not the heaven of revelation, therefore, that he looks for, who confines his adoration to the Father, or withholds his confidence from the blood of the Lamb. For, what part could he take in hallelujahs, which glorify God and the Lamb equally; or in anthems, which ascribe salvation entirely and exclusively to the blood of atonement? This is the worship of heaven; and it swells equally from the hearts and harps of saints and angels. What, therefore could a Unitarian do there, but either confess that he had never believed the bible; or charge all heaven with idolatry and error? This would be, in fact, his only alternative. He could do nothing, but acknowledge himself to have been a fool on earth, or impeach the whole "general assembly" of saints and angels, as idolaters.

Is it not, therefore, unmanly, yea mean, even to contemptibleness, to talk of heaven, and yet to treat Christ as a mere man and a martyr, It cannot, surely, be the heaven of revelation, which Unitarians mean, when they speak of a glorious immortality; for *"the Lamb is the light and glory"* of the Immortality illuminated by the gospel: and, if they do mean another heaven, why do they not speak out, and tell us plainly where and what it is? Those should not mystify, who denounce mystery!

After this, never pretend that you know not what creed to adopt. If you desire to spend your eternity in the heaven which the Savior opened in the visions of Patmos, and announced in his sermons, adopt the creed of that heaven. Adore God and the Lamb, as all the armies of it do; and thus you can never be at a loss. There will, indeed, still be mystery—much and great mystery; but all of it openly sanctioned by all who are around the throne, and by *"Him that sitteth on the throne."*

Look now at the second fact. All the verdicts of experience accredit Trinitarianism, as *"the truth as it is in Jesus."* All fulfilling prophecy, and all signal Providences, are on its side. The mysterious creed is, thus, the only form of Christianity which has ever been successful or sanctifying in our world. Weigh this fact. Prophecy supposes and requires the existence and exercise of a special Providence, in order to its fulfilment; and an overruling Providence, once established, opens such a guardianship for truth in the world, that we may naturally expect to find the latter under the wing of the former, and the wheel of Providence in the track of the gospel, breaking up its way amongst the nations, and gradually crushing down opposition. Now, if Unitarianism be "the truth as it is in Jesus," it, and it alone, will exhibit on its side, all the signal interpositions of Providence since the Christian era. For, if they have been on the side of Trinitarianism, God, on Unitarian principles, has been giving currency to error and success to absurdity. This hint will prepare you for the following part of this essay; in which I will endeavor to show you that there is no alternative but denying a special Providence altogether, or admitting that, hitherto, it has been exercised in behalf of Trinitarianism, and against Unitarianism.

I have recourse to this argument, not only because it is conclusive, but because it is simple and more suited than critical disquisitions, to all capacities. Every person is familiar with the doctrine of an overruling Providence, and in the habit of expecting the hand of God on the side of his own cause. This is as it should be, and a happy circumstance for one of the creeds. Truth, you will allow, is an important thing in any state of society; and never was more wanted than at the time when Christ began to promulgate it to the world. Error was then triumphant, and stood Colossus-like, with one foot on Mars Hill, and the other on the Tarpeian mount. Her right hand rested on the pyramids of Egypt—and her left on the pillars of Hercules; around her gigantic form, wreathed the incense of ten thousand altars; her embossed pedestal was purpled with blood, and her shrine hung with the shields of the mighty, and the harps of antiquity. Beneath the shadow of her wings, lay the tombs of generations, sculptured with every emblem but immortality—and her temples, whilst they enchanted the eye, lent all their charms to licentiousness and fiction.

Such was the sway and fascination of error, when Truth, in the meek and lowly form of a servant, sat down on the Mount of Olives to teach mankind. A few indigent fishermen were her first adherents, and, until the splendor of her miracles gave éclat to her doctrines, her "gracious words" could hardly redeem her from public contempt. But her cause was heaven's cause—and heaven interfered to vindicate it, by enabling Truth to wield the elements, at will—to bind death and diseases in chains—and to reap her trophies on every field of misery and despair. And this she did successfully. But I forget: personification is admissible only in an oration, and I am writing an essay. In plain terms, then, Providence smiled upon the sermons of Christ and his apostles, and made subsiding storms, retiring disorders, and opening graves, the harbingers and pioneers of the gospel. The eyes of the blind were opened to behold its heralds— the ears of the deaf unstopped to hear them—the tongues of the dumb unloosed to hail them—the understanding of the weak enabled to comprehend them; until the world witnessed classes of the unfortunate, once unfit to take any part in the form of religion, exclaiming in the spirit of it, *"How beautiful on the mountains are the feet of them that preach the gospel of peace, and bring glad tidings of good things."*

Thus the ministry of reconciliation was introduced with a degree of glory that excelled even the splendid patronage under which Judaism opened. The rocks of Gennesaret were made as famous as Baalzephon —the Mount of Olives vied with Horeb, and Calvary became more monumental than Sinai. Miracles made every element and every obstacle tributary to the cause of truth. By such "signs and wonders," God taught the world to expect, that the gospel never would be left without a witness of some kind. And the expectation thus awakened, was not weakened in the least, even when miracles were withdrawn; but the church continued to calculate, as sanguinely, upon support and countenance from on High, when the pentecostal tongues of fire became extinct, as when they glowed in all the freshness of novelty; because the moment miracles ceased, the visions of prophecy began; opening a vista through futurity, illuminated at every point by the bright and morning Star—and terminated only by the great white throne and the brink of eternity.

God did not more signally prove Himself by miracles, to be on the side of truth, them. He solemnly pledged Himself, by prophecy, to continue on its side forever. Is He, then, has He ever been, on the side of Unitarianism? If so—when, where, how? The right hand of God is not such an indefinite or indistinct object, but it may be pointed to, when it is stretched out in His own cause. He has made it bare, in the sight of all nations: successive ages have said of successive interpositions, "Is not this the finger of God?" And, at this moment, the Christian world feel themselves on the verge of a moral era, the very dawn of which sets them on tiptoe as they gaze. And, has Unitarianism neither part nor lot in this matter? Is she *"like the heath in the desert,"* that knoweth not when good comes? Seriously, this hint begins to wear a dark aspect on that cause. It is nigh time for Unitarians to collect witnesses: for I should think they could not sleep, until like Ahasuerus, they *"commanded to bring the book of the Chronicles,"* of the Unitarian kingdom. Or shall I save them the trouble, by stating at once, that there has been nothing to register, but disasters and defeats? Of late, indeed, their system has obtained a name and place in the old Presbyterian chapels of England; but how was possession gained? Tell it not in Gath!—under the mask of orthodoxy—by means you would not connect Providence with, nor attempt to sanctify by their success. And, as this event stamps indelible disgrace upon those

Unitarians, who "with feigned words made merchandise" of the Trinitarian congregations— where are the interpositions of Providence on behalf of the new system.

But I forget: it claims, of course, all the miraculous and signal interpositions of Providence, during the first and second centuries; since, according to its own account, Unitarianism was the primitive system. Now, suppose I grant this, for a moment, for the sake of argument, what does it lead to? In fact, to a conclusion which, of itself, disproves the assumption. For, if it were true, that all the miracles were wrought in behalf of Unitarianism, it would be true, also, that all the prophecies were written in its behalf: but as none of the latter have been fulfilled in its favor, none of the former belong to it—because, both must be found on one side, or not at all. Granting again, however, that it was Unitarianism, which was ushered into the world amidst the songs of angels, and under the banners of miracles; that for it, a highway was opened into "Cesar's household," and all across the moral wilderness of the three continents; how comes it that God abandoned Unitarianism, when the banners of miracles were folded up? How do you account for its triumphs ceasing ever since, and its being left to the scorn of every church and state in Christendom Why is it, that everything known or acknowledged as Providence, has, since the failure of miracles, frowned on that creed?

This is not the manner of the Most High, in regard to truth—this is not what we are taught to expect from his management. God, (if Unitarianism were the gospel), has been harassing and depressing the gospel, for fifteen hundred years, and making every vicissitude and revolution abet the cause of error. I will allow all the weight you please, to the success of Unitarianism in America—in Geneva–in England: this token for good shall be as good, as Unitarians choose to call it; as encouraging as they say. Yes, weave their laurels into all the width of surface, which their greenness and length will go to; they are but shoots of yesterday, on both sides of the Atlantic. Now, this ought not to be the case—if they are the laurels of truth. Besides, if God has any hand in the recent success of that sect, how do you account for his hand being withdrawn during fifteen hundred years? Were you to claim, even the age of Sociniusism, as the era when the primitive truth was revived, there would be still an awful series of ages between that and the third century —and in none of them, can you discern Truth and Providence together. I multiply and press such questions, because the doctrine of an overruling Providence seems fully recognized by some of their best writers. Dr. Rees, in his oration, delivered on laying the first stone of the Old Jewry Chapel, says of the system: "It is under the protection of the God of nature and providence: and we are assured by the Word of divine truth that the gates of Hades shall not prevail against it. Providence will raise in this place, and in other places of a similar kind, a succession of those who will retain and avouch the principles of their fathers. The stone which is now to be fixed in its proper place, will, I trust, be an emblem not only of the durability of this edifice, but of the permanency of the society to which it belongs. It will, in this respect, resemble that rock on which the founder of our Christian faith hath built his church."

These are excellent sentiments; but, were they not equally true and applicable, when the foundation stones of the primitive chapels were laid: Had not the Rees's of that age, when according to the Rees's of this age, Unitarianism was orthodoxy, a right to calculate on Providence "raising up a succession of those who should retain and avouch the principles of their fathers? Such a succession, however, were not raised up until Sociniusism appeared. This single fact, therefore, is fatal either to the doctrine of Providence, or to the pretensions of Unitarians. Which of the two, then, will they give up as untenable; for both they cannot retain. I leave Unitarians to adjust these jarring events—and proceed to remind you of the triumphs of that system—the doctrines of which are mysterious. I have granted, for the sake of argument, that Unitarianism might be the primitive system: and we have seen that it was soon forsaken by Providence. Now, only pay me back the compliment for a moment, and grant that Trinitarianism was the primitive system; and if you find that forsaken by Providence, in any age since the Christian era, I will admit that you have established a serious objection against it. Assuming, them, that Trinitarianism was the system taught by Christ and his apostles, the sudden death of Constantine saved it from the deep-laid scheme of Eusebius to establish Arianism in its room. Constans maintained it in the western empire, until he was murdered. Constantius could not stifle it—nor Julian sneer it into contempt—nor Valens eradicate it—nor Apollinaris corrupt it. Even, whilst the imperial scepter was shifting like a shadow, from hand to hand, and the state of religion modelling according to state policy, Trinitarianism held its place, from the time of Constantine till that of Theodosius, when it became dominant, and has continued so ever since. It became encumbered, indeed, under a succession of popes, with a load of folly and extravagance; caught a form of absurdity and a spirit of fire, and appeared on the seven hills of Rome more like a destroying angel than a messenger of peace. These fiery elements, however, which glowed around Trinitarianism then, were not fed from the bosom of its radical doctrines, but issued from the volcanoes of ecclesiastical ambition. In proof of this, I appeal to the system since it has been disentangled by the reformers.

Luther snatched it from the electric atmosphere of Rome; Calvin, from the feudalism of the Germanic electors; Knox from the clanship of the Scotch; Cromwell from the teeth of the Stuarts; and, now that it is still farther disencumbered by the Orthodox, it is both tolerant and benevolent. It is the fact, therefore, that ever since Trinitarianism, like a vessel, was launched from the port of Judea upon the sea of public opinion, she has not only rode out every storm, during eighteen centuries, but touched at every shore, and colonized every island. It will not do, in the face of all this, for Unitarians to affect composure, and exclaim "Truth is great and will prevail." Truth has always been great—and her greatness of that kind which has always insured, what their system never had—the smiles of Providence. And it would be still worse, to evade these arguments by saying that Unitarianism has had but a short time for her experiments on the world. It has been brief, certainly: but the shorter you prove it to be—the longer you make the period during which Providence abandoned and overthrew what they call "The Truth."

If the foregoing remarks illustrate anything to the point, it is, that public opinion, prophecy, and Providence wear an equally unfavorable aspect towards Unitarianism. Public opinion braves the system—prophecy brands it Antichrist—Providence which forms public opinion and fulfils prophecy, abandons their cause upon every great movement of the moral world.

I come, now, to the manifest inconsistency between the tenor of Scripture and the tenor of Unitarianism. And, as my limits impose the utmost brevity, I must have recourse to a mode of illustration, which will give *multum in parvo*. Unitarianism is a system—and according to Unitarians, a perfect summary of the revealed will of God to man for the obedience of faith. Now, if it be a perfect digest of divine truth, (and it ought to be so before urging it on the world), it wants nothing but the formal authority of the bible, to make it equal to the bible. For, if a transfer of that authority to the system did not raise it to an equal rank with the Scriptures—it could only be, because it is unscriptural in its present state. They say—it is not; and cannot say otherwise, without giving up its claims. Suppose, then, for a moment, that God, in a visible and indisputable manner, should abolish the bible entirely, and give to the world, in its stead, a written copy of the Unitarian system, having all the authority and sacredness which the bible has had. You know, that God could do so, and by a few signal miracles, stamp the divinity of the latter, as high as the former. Suppose all this done, in the eyes of all nations; and the creed of every nation Unitarian; and this state of things five hundred years old; and the present bible utterly forgotten; and the existing commentaries and orthodox writings lost; and nothing extant but what Unitarians approve of now. They can have no serious objections to these suppositions, because the chief part of them are hopes they cherish, and wish to see realized.

Now, suppose that after five hundred years, (when their system would be dominant, and endeared by as many pious and learned works, as Trinitarianism now boasts) some minister of talents and influence, should address such a circular, as the following, to the Unitarian churches:

Dearly Beloved,

Grace be with you, mercy, and peace from God the Father, and from the Lord Jesus Christ, the Son of the Father, in truth and love. All men should honor the Son, even as they honor the Father. And let all the angels of God worship him—for he is before all things, and by Him all things consist. By Him were all things created, that are in heaven, and that are in earth, visible and invisible, whether they be thrones, or dominions, or principalities, or powers: all things were made by Him, and for Him. His goings forth were of old, even from everlasting. When His Father addressed Him, He said, "Thy throne, O God, is forever and ever! Thou, Jehovah, in the beginning didst lay the foundation of the earth: and the heavens are the works of thy hand." Therefore, it becomes us to ascribe, "Blessing, and honor, and glory and power, unto Him that sitteth on the throne, and unto the Lamb forever and ever: because, he that honoreth not the Son, honoreth not the Father. The grace of our Lord Jesus Christ be with you all. Amen.

How would such a letter be received by churches formed on the principle, that divine names and divine honors, are the exclusive rights of the Father? The writer would be branded as an idolater, and his letter committed to the flames. Or, if any one leaned to his opinions—an appeal would be made to the New Bible, (which I have supposed), and the wavering brother dared to produce from it, one instance in which Christ is called God, Jehovah, or Creator. And you know that he could not, if any of the existing summaries of Unitarianism were exalted in the rank of the Bible, and substituted in its room. And if these passages, which I have thrown into the form of a letter, would savor of idolatry, five hundred years hence, (under that state of things, I have supposed) they do so now, on every principle, but that of the Son's equality with the Father. Thus, there is no alternative but to embrace mystery, or to succumb to absurdity. Even Deists see this, and laugh at the farce of retaining the Bible, and discarding mystery.

8

On Manly Views of Divine Holiness

The most natural and scriptural idea we can form of the divine life and blessedness, *"from everlasting,"* is, that the past eternity was occupied in planning what will take the future eternity to accomplish. And now, observe—the infinite holiness of Jehovah was the basis of His infinite happiness from everlasting. God has been blessed forever, because holy forever; for on no other ground could eternal happiness rest or remain. It has been often proved, to demonstration, that if God had not always been, He never could have been at all: and it is equally capable of demonstration that if He had not been always holy, he never could have been happy. This fact is self-evident, when viewed in connection with the eternity which preceded all created being and things; for then, besides Himself, there was nothing to delight in, or to be occupied with. If, therefore, the eternal mind was not of a character to find enjoyment in itself, and to be the spring of its own felicity, it had no resource whatever beyond itself—and must have been miserable. I repeat it— God must from everlasting have been miserable, if not immaculately holy from everlasting; because prior to the birth of time, there were no external sources of enjoyment: and internal there could not have been, if purity was wanting; because, in that case, there was no security against bad feelings—which are their own punishment. Mind, whether created or uncreated, is of such a nature, that it cannot cease from thinking or feeling about itself or something; and in proportion to its power is its activity.

Now the powers of the eternal Mind being infinite, must have been infinitely active: and if active only or even often about evil—conscious misery, in the same degree, must have been the consequence. I dare not trust myself to follow out this argument; but I see, at a glance, how an unholy God must be a wretched being, exactly in proportion to His intellectual energy. Such a being might annihilate himself, or become insane, during the height and sweep of infinite passions. But I check my own mind: the true God is essentially and infinitely holy; and therefore has been eternally happy. No wrong thought or feeling ever passed through His mind; but, from everlasting, its powers circle around its plans, calm and bright as the sea of glass around the throne of glory. And what must the holiness of the divine nature be, seeing it has forever maintained the balance and harmony of infinite energies, although all in external exercise; upheld from everlasting the tranquility and equanimity of that mind, through which all the affairs of all worlds —of all beings—of all time—of all eternity, have passed in revision, deliberation, and judgment.

This mighty sum of beings, things, and events, even if all uniformly lovely in themselves, seem too immense to be contemplated with unmixed pleasure or unfailing patience:— and, diversified as they are by vice and weakness, it seems impossible to have even thought of them all, without passion or pain. And, without being glorious in holiness, God could not have viewed them, unimpaired in His own happiness: but, strange to tell!—holiness, the very perfection which makes evil abhorrent to God, is the very perfection which from eternity upheld His bliss and composure in contemplating all things. These are wonderful themes, if we only had strength to follow them up to their height: but even as bare hints, they are inspiring to reflecting minds. I love to get disentangled from time, and the checkered scenes of life, until I live, in thought, before them all. I cannot shake off the perplexities occasioned by the aspect of nature and providence, until I get beyond their birth, and into the solitary depths of a silent eternity:—but, them, although in one sense lost, in another I am found, by simple facts; by solid principles; by self-evident maxims, which, like guardian angels, take me by the hand, and conduct me into marvelous light, and peace unspeakable.

If you can hardly believe this, I will give you a specimen of reasoning—the eternity before time. I enter it looking for the throne of God: I find the high and holy place: I am assured that the Holy One has dwelt there from eternity, glorious in holiness! And now, I want no more to reason from. On this basis, I can build up the theory of the universe He is to create, and of the government He is to establish. Thus: will a God infinitely holy, rise from His eternal throne to make anything evil? No. To do anything evil? No. To act contrary to His nature? No. To tarnish His unsullied purity? No. Then, let the universe of being rise when it will; let His system of government be promulgated when it may: all will be right—all as it should be; for the Author of all is glorious in holiness. Men and things may be mysterious, changeable, checkered, in their lot, aspect, and character; but whatever evil there may be in either, a Holy God cannot be the author of it.

Having got hold of this self-evident and certain truth, I bring it down to the fall of the angels: they are miserable in all their immortal powers: no wonder; they are unholy; and un-holiness would make God Himself miserable. Even His happiness could not survive the loss of His holiness; how then could theirs? I now apply the principle to mankind: misery, both natural and moral, abounds in the world; all men are more or less unhappy at all times: they search creation for happiness in vain, and find only vexation of spirit. This seems hard; but they are unholy; and therefore inevitably unhappy. God Himself could not avoid being wretched, were He unholy. His creatures are, therefore, even in the depths of their wretchedness, only what He Himself must be, were He like them in heart and character. Here then I deny that there is any mystery in the severest dispensations of Providence, if you admit that there is sin in all that suffer by them. While men are unholy, they must be unhappy: this consequence is as natural and inevitable, as darkness after sunset, or cold in winter. Now the sum of divine holiness has held an eternal meridian; and, therefore, God has been blessed forever; but the sun of human holiness has set; and, therefore, men are unhappy. In the case of the children of God, that sun is rising again, and, therefore, they are rising again to enjoyment and peace; but not until it shine in perfect day, will either be perfect.

Away, therefore, with the unprincipled clamor about hard lots, heavy calamities, mysterious trials: I have had my share of them; but I see nothing unfair or unaccountable in them. Those, therefore, who only condole and sympathize with sufferers, defeat their own kind purpose: for the misery they strive to mitigate, admits of no effectual cure but restoration to true holiness, or the image of God. While, therefore, I wish my heart to be like the river sponge, saturated with the passing streams of another's sorrow, and weeping with those that weep, I must belie all right principle, if I do not feel chiefly for their and my own want of holiness.

Having thus given you some idea of how essential holiness is even to the happiness of God, you will now be prepared to go fully into the subject of this essay. His holiness is represented as the beauty of His nature and character. Even Plutarch, the heathen philosopher, obtained, somehow, a glimpse of this fact, and said, "Holiness is the beauty of the divine essence; God is not so happy by an eternity of life, as by excellency of virtue." Proclus calls God, "the undefiled Governor of the world." And it was to keep this beauty of the divine nature untarnished, that some of the wisest of the heathen writers invented the eternity of matter: to that, they ascribed all sim, that they might acquit God of being the author of sin: so sacred was their idea of His holiness. In like manner, to absolve God from all taint or suspicion of evil, the Manichean heretics maintained two eternal principles; the one the origin of all evil, the other the origin of all good : thus running into absurdities in order to avoid that contradiction in terms, an unholy God. Now, if heathens and heretics were thus careful to invest God with the beauty of holiness, we may expect that the sacred writers would not neglect to do so. Accordingly Jehosaphat summons all the vocal and instrumental powers of music, to the theme, that they might praise the beauty of holiness. To behold the beauty of the Lord, David desired to dwell in the house of the Lord forever. To illustrate it, he represents Jehovah clothed with light as a garment. In like manner, both the Old and New Testament writers agree in exhibiting the divine holiness as the beauty, which captivates and charms all the armies of heaven: *"they rest not day nor night, crying, Holy, holy, holy, Lord God Almighty."*

Thus while the Bible calls the omnipotence of God His arm; His omniscience His eye; His mercy His heart; His infinity His form; His eternity His life; they call His holiness His beauty. And, agreeably to this fine idea, that beauty is made to beautify, with its own reflected loveliness, everything it relates to. This is so well illustrated by a living writer, that I cannot do so well as to quote his own words: "Because heaven is the habitation of the holy God, it is called His holy heaven: because the temple was the place where He graciously afforded the indications of His presence, it was called His holy temple: the very ground on which Jehovah condescended to admit Moses to an audience, was called holy ground : the mountain on which the Savior was transfigured was called the holy mount : the day set apart for divine worship is called the holy day: and in a far higher sense are the people of God called a holy people." I will only add to this fine enumeration, the unparalleled emblem of David, where he describes the beauty of the holiness of the Savior's people, as *"the dew from the womb of the morning."* And if their infinite and reflected holiness will be eventually as the morning dew; with what beauty must infinite and essential purity invest Jehovah?

Well may it be said the heavens are not clean in His sight. His holiness is represented as the glory of His nature, character, and government. It is on this principle that God celebrates His justice as holy justice; His wisdom as holy wisdom; His omnipotence as His holy arm; His omniscience as His holy eye; His truth as His holy promise; His commands as His holy law; and all His works as holy works. Thus He is altogether glorious in holiness: for, without that, says Charnock, His patience would be indulgence to sin, His mercy a fondness, His wrath a madness, His power a tyranny, His wisdom a subtlety. His holiness gives a decorum to all.

"Were not all His perfections distinguished and adorned by the quality of holiness," says Dr. Burder, "He who sways the scepter of the universe might be an object of dread, but not of love or confidence. Such a being might become the scourge and terror of creation." This is, indeed, strong language; but I quote it without apology, because if I employed my own upon the subject it would be far stronger without being less true; for if anything be morally certain, it is that without holiness there would be no real glory in any one of the divine perfections, because no security for their rational or fair exercise. It is not, however, necessary to pursue this argument farther: let us therefore satisfy ourselves that holiness is the glory of all the divine perfections. To prove and illustrate this fact in the case of each attribute of Jehovah would occupy more space than I can command; I will therefore confine my remarks to His mercy and justice; for these two virtually include all the rest.

Now, holiness is the glory of divine mercy, whether that mercy be viewed as the disposition of God, the purpose of God, or the act of God: in all these characters, it has its chief glory in its holiness. And, in this way: mercy viewed as the disposition of Jehovah, or as His feelings, flows from His love of holiness; for had He not loved that supremely and unspeakably He would have felt no sympathy for sinners, but would have allowed them to be unholy still. Had He cared nothing, or but little about holiness, He would have had no motive nor inclination to provide a Savior; for of what consequence could it be, however vile man were, if God were indifferent about purity? But because He loved purity infinitely, He so loved the world as to give His only begotten Son to be the Propitiation for sin and the Redeemer from sin. His mercy, in its principle, plan, and gift, is, therefore, the measure of His love to Holiness; because the practical design of all his mercy is, to bring around

His throne, in the beauty of holiness, a multitude which no man can number; all without spot or blemish.

That His people may be holy as He is holy, He made His Son unto them, "wisdom, righteousness, and sanctification." Thus every step, struggle, sacrifice and triumph of mercy on behalf of man was on behalf of holiness too; love to the latter furnished the motive, inflamed the desire, fortified the resolution and found the means of redeeming the former. Holiness is therefore the glory of mercy. The plan of mercy is a holy covenant; the Mediator of mercy, a holy Savior; the Applier of mercy, a holy Spirit; the fruits of mercy, a holy generation; the final glory of mercy, a church like unto Him Who is the express image of the Father of mercies. Well, therefore, may I call upon myself and you, in the language of Jehosaphat, *"Praise ye the beauty of holiness,"* and in the language of David, *"Give thanks at the remembrance of God's holiness."* Well may we charge our souls to love holiness supremely; for had not God loved it so, He would not have so loved the world as to give His Son to save His people from their sins.

I must not quit this part of the subject, without availing myself of the fine opportunity it affords of attaching distinct ideas to the general maxim that the cause of all that God has done in salvation is simply the advancement of his own glory. Nothing can be more true than this maxim; but let not your ideas of its meaning be vague. The glory of Jehovah is His goodness. Why? Just because holiness is the foundation and spring of all His goodness. He is good because He is holy; for to spread, exalt, and perpetuate holiness throughout the universe, His tender mercies are over all His other works. We do not, therefore, go far enough when we trace redemption to the love of God as its first cause; and to the glory of God as its final end. That ought to be done, cannot be too often done; but whenever it is done there is another thing that should not be left undone: namely, tracing the love of God to its origin or moral cause; which is the holiness of the divine nature, or God's love of righteousness. Nothing can be more certain than this; for an unholy God could neither have motive nor inclination to love the world in the way the High and Holy One has done. Here then are distinct ideas of His glory being the final end of all His works; it is the promotion of holiness by the exercise of goodness.

Allow me therefore to indulge my feelings for a moment here, and to say, "Holiness thou art the fountain of all the love, the grace, the mercy, and the goodness which are to us the fountains of salvation. Thou art the foundation of all the kindness, condescension, and faithfulness which are to us the foundations of hope and confidences. Thou art the shield of the unchangeableness, truth and omnipotence, which are to us the shields of eternal safety and protection. Give thanks at the remembrance of Thy holiness. Yes, Holy One of Israel, never will I forget it; never remember it without regarding it as the eternal source and the eternal security of all that is gracious in Thy heart, glorious in Thy character, wonderful in Thy works. Because Thou art infinitely holy, Thou art infinitely good; because Thou wilt be eternally holy, Thou wilt be eternally good. I have thought of Thy holiness with suspicion or hatred: so foolish was I that I have wished Thee less holy! This was in fact wishing Thee to be my implacable and immortal enemy forever; wishing myself and Thee to be eternally wretched. "Thus I was as a beast before Thee!" I have heard of Thee by the hearing of the ear, but now mine eye seeth Thee; wherefore I abhor myself and repent in dust and ashes."

I proceed now to show how holiness is the glory of divine justice. Every act of justice on the part of God is only the exercise of holiness, however summary, severe, or final. The same holiness originates and regulates all judgment, which originated and regulates all mercy. As God does not go a step farther in pardoning than where He can be holy in doing so, neither will He in punishing. He will be glorious in holiness, both in saving and condemning. It is therefore well for devil and for all the lost that God is holy; for, though His being so must, in their case, prevent mercy, it will forever prevent injustice too. Nothing unnecessary or unreasonable ever has been, or ever will be, inflicted upon them. God will be holy in all His ways, including His justice. Holiness will preside, with the same equity over the end of sin as over bliss in heaven.

True, it may be said, but of what advantage will this be to condemned? It will afford them no pretext for charging God with injustice; for He will render unto every man only according to his works. Mark, then, the glory of justice in punishing sin; that, He will indulge no undue anger, inflict no unreasonable punishment. And yet, you say, the result of the punishment will be eternal. Yes, if anything less could avenge sin sufficiently, depend upon it Holiness would not have chosen it. It was in no passion, in no rash moment, that God decreed this as the penalty of sin. He was never more calm, collected, deliberate, or just, than when He understood this, as the sentence of the law, and the sanction of the Gospel: and He will be equally so when He executes that sentence. Let, therefore, no trifler flatter himself with the hope of entire escape, or of enduring less than destruction, if he persist in trifling with the Gospel. It cannot be less, except God become unholy; and, were He to become so, then ten thousand times woe to thee, beyond the woe of hell! Oh if I durst pour out the fullness of my own thoughts, and tell you what an unholy God must be, I could terrify you at the bare idea. Letting loose the planets from their orbits, and the sums of the universe from their centers, until the material creation was dashing to atoms, like icebergs in the shock of a polar storm in the northern seas, would be nothing to the letting loose of infinite power and passion, from the magnetic control of holiness. But on this point I promised to forbear; and I will, were it only in mercy to my own strained and startled imagination.

Having thus largely shown the light in which the Word of God places the holiness of God, I solicit your attention to the light in which the actual dispensations or works of God place His holiness. Now there are three classes of God's public measures, each of which manifests His immaculate holiness. There are His retributive, redeeming and regenerating works. I notice first His acts of judicial retribution or punishment; and here it deserves special observation that in Scripture the holiness of Jehovah is chiefly celebrated by saints and angels whenever any signal judgment is inflicted upon the wicked. It was just after the overthrow of the Egyptians in the Red Sea, and when they had sunk as lead in the mighty waters, that Moses and Miriam sang, *"Who is a God like unto thee, glorious in holiness."* It was while the temple shook and the judicial curse of a seared conscience went forth upon the Jews that the Seraphim cried one to another, *"Holy, holy, holy, Lord God of hosts, the whole earth is filled with thy glory."* It was when the Lord said, *"my determination is to gather the nations and assemble the kingdoms, that I may pour out my indignation, even all my fierce anger upon Jerusalem,"* it was then, Zephaniah said, *"the just Lord is in the midst thereof; he will do no iniquity."*

It is when the apocalyptic trumpets and thunders are sounding, and while the vials of wrath are pouring out on the seat of the beast and of the false prophet, that all who stand on the sea of glass, having the harps of God, sing, *"just and true are thy ways thou king of saints, thou only art holy."* Other instances might be quoted, but these will show that the most signal acts of judgment are viewed and adored by saints and angels as glorious manifestations of holiness. This fact agrees with and confirms the definition I gave of holiness as being that principle of the eternal mind by which God necessarily loves whatever is right, and hates whatever is wrong. Accordingly in punishing sin, God manifests his holiness, by proving his hatred of what is wrong. The most signal proof of this, in the case of creatures, was given in the final expulsion from Heaven of the angels who kept not their first estate. From thrones of light they were banished to chains of darkness; from being morning stars amongst the sons of God they were turned into meteors of devouring fire. The place on the hills of immortality, which knew them once, knows and will know them no more forever. They fell to rise no more; were cast out never to be taken in again. This act is usually called one of awful sovereignty; and, when contrasted with the treatment given to fallen man, it is the severity of sovereignty: but, viewed as it should be, by itself and in itself, I deny that it is anything of the kind. It was essentially and simply an act of perfect holiness; having in it not an iota of more severity than the demerits of the case absolutely demanded. Those who will not take the trouble of thinking may talk nonsense if they choose; and resolve unpitied sufferings into unmixed sovereignty; it is an easy process, a convenient abyss for burying difficulties in.

I believe in a God infinitely holy. I must, therefore, either maintain that He is unholy, or that the punishment of fallen angels is the very least, in mature and degree, that a holy God could inflict, and yet maintain His holiness untarnished. If He could have abated a fraction of the penalty, or mitigated their curse, He would have done it. He would have rejoiced to do it! He would have been more prompt to lessen the weight of His wrath against sinning angels than they could have been in asking for a diminution of it. In their punishment there is as perfectly a holy act in its principle and character as God's approving and accepting the perfect work of His own Son. There was no more passion in the way He treated them than there was partiality in the way He treated Christ. Away therefore with all equivocating and evasion; if God be holy, nothing but holiness shines in the fate of fallen angels. Accordingly they themselves acknowledge as much to Christ. *"Let us alone; art thou come to torment us before our time. We know thee, who thou art, thou Holy One of God."* Thus they insinuated no charge of injustice or of sovereignty as marking their doom; but merely asked for exemption from the fullness of their torment until the fullness of its time.

If you have been thinking that all this is useless speculation upon a point foreign to our interests, you will soon find yourself in a mistake. I am not speculating, but speaking forth the words of truth and soberness, concerning the holiness of God. And now mark; there will be nothing but holiness, in the act of putting to an end all the wicked. There will be no undue severity in their doom. It will be just what the interests and claims of holiness require, and nothing more or less. Men may talk of this as horror, and shocking, and severe; but, if such epithets implicate either the justice or the goodness of God, they are as foolish as they are impious, unless it be a horrid and shocking thing that God should be holy. He must become unholy, or the punishment of sin must be final. There is no other alternative. But do you not see that if God became unholy, eternal misery would be equally sure then as it is now;

because an unholy being would actually take delight in spreading and perpetuating misery. Wretched himself, he would go about as a roaring lion through the universe seeking whom he might devour; regardless of character or circumstances. The hell of the Bible is, therefore, the least of the two evils. What, then, must the holiness of Jehovah be, seeing that nothing less than complete destruction is its sentence against the unholy; seeing this is the very least punishment that God can inflict and remain holy Himself?

I know not how this view of the solemn fact may affect your minds; but for my own part, I must say, that since I saw it in this light I dread it ten thousand times more than ever I did; for now there is no mystery about the principle on which God acts toward the unholy; no secret or sovereign reason for His finality; no passion in his procedure; but hell is simply the natural consequence of holiness in the Creator, and un-holiness in the creature, and the Creator's desire to restore holiness and community between the redeemed and Himself. As it was in the beginning, so shall it be in the end. *And God shall wipe every tear from their eyes; and there shall be no more death, neither sorrow nor crying.*

Here, my lips are shut; my reasoning silenced forever, because I see that God can do nothing less than end sin. Whatever others do, therefore, as for me, I will seek escape from that end by the Sacrifice provided for me, which glorified the divine holiness in the highest; for in no other way have I any hope.

I notice next—The redeeming acts of God, as manifesting his immaculate holiness. We have already seen that, if anything be morally certain, it is that an unholy God would be unmerciful; because, were He unholy, He must be infinitely so, and therefore could neither be just nor kind. Such a Being could have no motive nor inclination to redeem from guilt and impurity sinful creatures: making them holy could never be a desirable end for Him to pursue; because were it accomplished it would exalt their character above His own, and thus inevitably subject him to their abhorrence. But, do you not see with equal clearness, that a God of infinite purity has powerful motives and glorious reasons for purifying the unholy? He is, indeed, under no necessity or obligation to yield to the force of these motives; but if He do so he acts worthy of Himself and manifests supreme love to holiness: for surely nothing could be more in harmony with His essential character than to assimilate the unholy to His own beautiful image. This is to multiply its reflections; and in the case of man to magnify its glory; because to restore lost holiness is a more glorious act than to impart original holiness. The very design of redeeming sinners is therefore a decisive and illustrious proof of the divine holiness; because the effect of redemption will be entire and eternal conformity to the divine image.

This perfection shines gloriously in the plan of redemption; that too, like the design of saving sinners, is a splendid illustration of Jehovah's holiness; for as a plan salvation is in harmony with every perfection of the Godhead, and every principle of the divine government. It provides not only for their vindication and entire satisfaction, but also for their eternal glory. Condescension made no stoop on behalf of man but upon the wings of holiness: mercy took no step but on the ground of holiness; wisdom no measures but on the maxims of holiness; grace no part but on the principles of holiness; love no interest but for the glory of holiness. The first thing settled and secured by the everlasting covenant was that God should be just; just to all His perfections, just to all His principles, just to all His eternal designs; and, that secured, He could then glorify Himself in justifying the ungodly who believe in Jesus. The difficulty of being a just God, once removed, He became with all his heart a Savior. Thus the plan of redemption proves His holiness. In like manner, the means and method of accomplishing salvation proves it.

The Son of God undertook to be the Mediator of the holy covenant, and thus became the voluntary victim of holiness in the room of the unholy. Never was this perfection so awfully or illustriously displayed as in the treatment of Christ. Holiness took the Son from the bosom of the Father—expelled Him from his seat upon the eternal throne—veiled His divine nature in a human body—banished Him for thirty years into the deep obscurity of the humblest life; and when all this was done, Holiness was only beginning to punish its victim. It brought Him from obscurity, as it brought Him from the Throne, and placed Him under the law of God and the lash of men and devils. Holiness led Him about Judea, homeless, friendless, destitute; and, though His heart was broken with reproaches, kept Him laboring for the good of His implacable enemies. Holiness exiled Him into the wilderness to be tempted of the devil and exhausted by fasting: again, it drew Him into public life and labor; and again thrust Him back into the solitude of the garden, to drink the cup of wrath.

Now, it roused Him from his bloody trance to at a heathen tribunal; anon, it tore off His garments rolled in blood and clothed Him in a robe of mockery. Now, it laid His cross upon His shoulders until He fainted; and anon, it nailed Him to the cross. Now, it hid the sun from His eyes; and anon, hid the light of His Father's countenance. Now, it made His soul an offering for sin; and anon, delivered His body to the grave. Then, and not until then, did holiness finish its avenging strokes upon the victim of law and justice. And in all this awful and heart-rending process there was nothing but holiness proceeding against sin. All this was the very least in kind, degree, and duration, that a holy God could inflict, if sin was to be atoned for, and His own character maintained. Not one feeling of cruelty, not an iota of excess, not a shadow of unnecessary severity marked any part of the Savior's sufferings.

The Savior himself is the best judge of the wrath He underwent. Observe how He explained it. Prophecy introduced Him saying, *"My God, my God, why hast Thou forsaken me? Why art Thou so far from helping me, and from the words of my roaring? O my God, I cry in the daytime, but Thou hearest not: and in the night season, and am not silent. But Thou art holy, O Thou that inhabits the praises of Israel."*

"But Thou art holy." Thus He was to acquit His Father of all undue severity: and He did, when He said, *"The cup which my Father gave me, shall I not drink it?"* He did more than acquit Him: He approved of, in the highest, all that He underwent. *"My meat and my drink is to do the will of Him that sent me."*

Here, then, was the holiness of God: He made Him who knew no sin, a sin offering for us, that we might be made the righteousness of God in Him. "Never surely," says one, "should we lose the impression of the holiness of God, were we for a single instant to hear that piercing cry, "I am tormented in this flame;" but still more affecting was the cry heard in Gethsemane, when in bitterest anguish of distress, the Son of God exclaimed, *"My soul is exceeding sorrowful even unto death."* Sinner, if a holy God could not spare His own holy Son, although his guilt was only imputed, and not personal, He will not— He cannot spare thee, if thou remainest unholy: and unholy thou wilt remain, if thou flee not to Christ for salvation.

And now observe how illustriously holiness was displayed in the acceptance and reward of the Savior's finished work. If God expressed His hatred of sin by the humiliation of His Son, by His exaltation He equally proved His love of holiness. The same principle regulated His proceedings in both cases. While the Savior was fulfilling all righteousness (that is, all holiness) by His obedience, the Holy Father could not conceal His love of this perfection; but exclaimed from the excellent glory, *"This is my beloved Son in whom I am well pleased."* When the Savior had become obedient unto death, even the death of the cross, God highly exalted Him—giving Him a name above every name. When he had seated Him upon the throne of the universe, amidst the homage and gratitude of all worlds, He explained it thus: *"Thou lovedst righteousness and hatedst iniquity, therefore God, even thy God, hath anointed thee with the oil of gladness."* Thus holiness goes the very same lengths in loving right, as in hating wrong.

The work of Christ, like the person of Christ, is perfectly holy; and therefore it meets with the perfection of the Father's delight. Yes; and sinners relying upon it for holy purposes will find the same acceptance. While God remains holy, the righteousness of his Son can never fail to justify in His sight all who are clothed with it. Paul was sure of this; and therefore counted all things but loss that he might be found in Christ.

I now notice the regenerating and sanctifying operations of God, as they illustrate His holiness. The immediate and remote object of all divine operations upon the heart of sinners is to renew them in righteousness and true holiness; to restore that beauty of holiness which was defaced by sin. And what a countless sum of these regenerating and sanctifying acts of the eternal Spirit are going forward at this moment. On what a variety of character, conditions and minds, are they operating! On the young and the old; the rich and the poor; the learned and the illiterate; the savage and civilized; and in all and each effecting the same change—from sin to holiness—from vice to virtue—from ungodliness to godliness. Wonderful Spirit! Thou art felt at once and alike here, and in all quarters of the globe; Thou art forever working on human hearts; and upon them all to implant and promote holiness. For this noble purpose a perpetual act of omnipotence has been going on in souls since the fall—is going on now—and will go on, until time be no more, and the church of the living God shall take her place before the throne without spot or blemish, holy as God is holy. And is He not holy, Who has thus appointed and employed the Holy Ghost to create, carry on, and perfect purity, in the souls of all the heirs of salvation? Is He not holy, Who conducts a special and perpetual Providence, every act of which has for its direct object to make believers conformed to his own holiness? If all things in nature clearly show the eternal power and Godhead; all things in Grace and Providence show to a certainty that God is glorious in holiness. Holy, holy, holy, Lord God of Hosts, the whole universe is full of Thy glory!

I have been thus very thorough on the subject of the Divine Holiness, because I never yet saw either a manly or a happy Christian amongst those who have but superficial views of that glory of the Divine character.

www.ingramcontent.com/pod-product-compliance
Lightning Source LLC
Chambersburg PA
CBHW070120080526
44586CB00013B/1344